SMOKE IN MIRRORS
Screenwriters Admit to Make-Believe!

I0603199

A report by

**Dr. Paul M Davies BA (hons.), MA, PhD,
AWGIES (3) Amateur Hypnotherapist**

This book is copyright. Apart from any fair dealing for the purpose of private study, research or review, as permitted under the Copyright Act, no part may be reproduced by any process without written permission.

© The moral right of the author has been asserted.

Interviews and articles in this book first appeared in *Metro, Cinema Papers* and *Cantrill's Filmnotes*.

Book Design   Tabitha Davies

First Edition
Gondwana Press
June 2020
Suffolk Park NSW 2481

Bringing the World
Back Together

CONTENTS

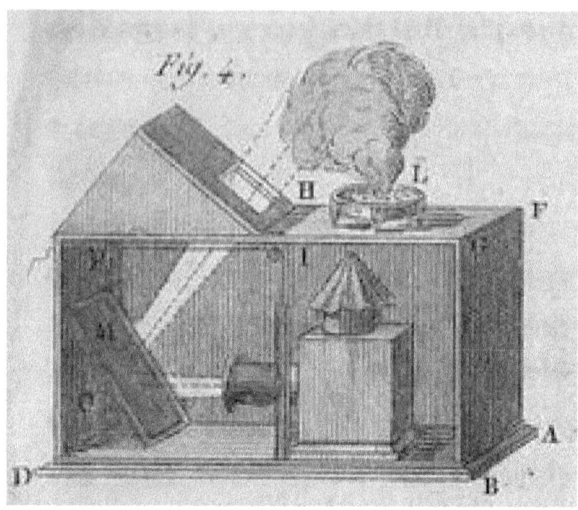

Projecting an image onto smoke with a mirror,
from *Nouvelles récréations physiques et mathématiques* (1770)

What goes on inside a screenwriter's head as they put words on a page for the purpose of producing moving images – sometimes with dialogue? Keith Thompson tries to conjure a "three dimensional image dancing". Peter Yeldham agrees it's "all in your mind". For Mark Shirrefs it's about a "different way of looking at things". Andrew Knight strives to get to "the heart of the matter". Roger Simpson searches for the "story engine". John Hughes works between "fact and fiction". Everett de Roche claims to be "only the writer". For Shane Maloney the stories are always about "crime, politics and the girl." And Elizabeth Huntley quite literally "hears voices".

All nine writers are talking about the art of make-believe, of 'holding the mirror up' - with sometimes a lot of smoke in the way. All were key players in a revival of Australian film and 'teledrama' that started in the early 1970s and continues to this day.

Some of their work includes classics such as: *Seachange, Homicide, The Sullivans, Neighbours, Patrick, Long Weekend, Ride On Stranger, Age of Consent, Touch And Go, The Sapphires, Clubland, Gail, The Girl From Tomorrow, Spellbinder, Stingers, Good Guys, Bad Guys, Halifax FP, What I Have Written, Film Work, Stiff, The Brush Off* and *Something In The Air*.

I'M ONLY THE WRITER
Everett de Roche
Cinema Papers **#25** (February-March 1980)

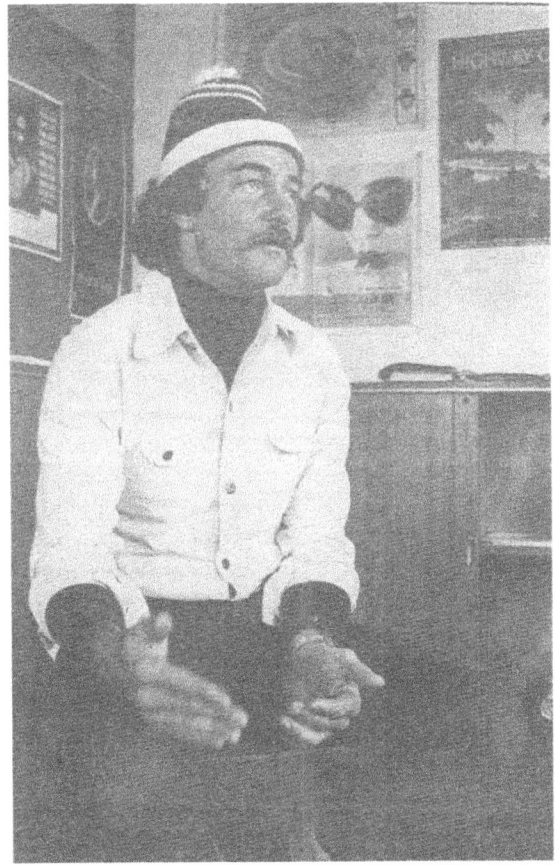

Everett de Roche at home in 1980

As the number of Australian Films produced since 1970 increases, so does the eagerness of critics to determine to what degree directors and scriptwriters have left their "auteurist" imprints. One scriptwriter who is receiving considerable critical scrutiny at the moment is Everett de Roche. Born in the U.S. in 1946, De Roche emigrated to Australia in the early 1970s (essentially to avoid being conscripted for the Vietnam war) and changed his name to "De Roche" as a kind of hippie joke. He began work as a journalist in Brisbane and then moved to Crawford Productions in Melbourne as a staff writer. Since going freelance, De Roche has written for television and the cinema. So far, four of his scripts have been filmed: *Patrick* (1978), *Long Weekend* (1978), *Snapshot* (1979), and *Harlequin* (1980). *Harlequin* was described by critic David Stratton as "inept and utterly absurd... the only Australian film that was utterly Americanised." On the other hand, Quentin Tarantino, who was inspired by "trash cinema" declared in 2008 that "everything Everett De Roche wrote is one of my favourite films."

Scenes from *Patrick* are actually echoed in American films like *Fatal Attraction* and (by his own admission) in Tarantino's *Kill Bill*. During the 1970s – the era of "Ozploitation" thrillers full of exploding cars and grisly murders - De Roche was the go-to writer. *Road Games* (1981) directed by Richard Franklin was written as a homage to Hitchcock's *Rear Window*. This was followed by *The Race for Yankee Zephyr* (1981) and *Razorback* (1984) – described as "*Jaws* with a wild boar in the Ozback". The film became a classic with fans of horror and suspense.

While at Crawfords, and for the princely sum of $250 each (five times what he earned as a journalist) De Roche wrote scripts for *Homicide, Matlock Police, Division 4, Bluey* and *Ryan* eventually earning $2,500 per episode. Later he wrote telemovies such as *Fortress* (1985) and *Windrider* (1986) and the original pilot for *Police Rescue*. Crawford producer Tony Cavanah described De Roche as the "most successful screenwriter in Australia – like an Australian Stephen King...he was also charming, funny and brilliant". However De Roche was far more than just a master of Ozploitation. His later work included scripts on internationally popular children's dramas: *Ship to Shore, Ocean Girl, Cyber Girl,* and *The Saddle Club*.

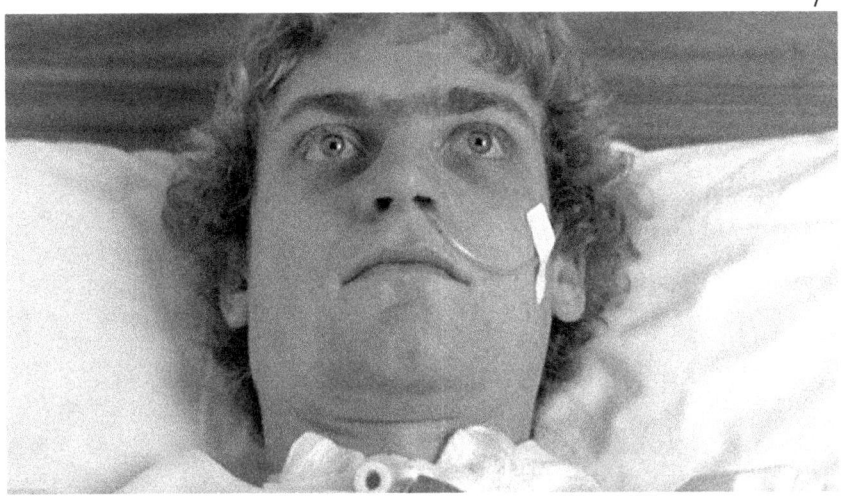

Robert Thompson as the comatose "Patrick"

Paul Davies: How long did it take to write *Patrick*?

Everett De Roche: The initial writing which I did three or four years ago took 10 days. That draft was 3 ½ hours long. It then became a matter of pruning it down. Once (director) Richard Franklin became involved there as even more re-writing.

Paul Davies: How different is the final script from your concept.

Everett De Roche: Originally it was a mystery where you were in doubt about what was happening. Richard made it a suspense-thriller and let the audience know from the start who the baddie was.

Paul Davies: *Patrick* deals with paranormal phenomena. Is that a theme you have wanted to write about?

Everett De Roche: Four years ago there weren't many films like *Patrick*. *The Exorcist* was about the only one. But between writing and completing the film a whole stack of occult-type films came out.

Paul Davies: Did this worry you?

Everett De Roche: Very much, because we would be accused of jumping on the bandwagon.

Paul Davies: To what degree did you research the script?

Everett De Roche: Most of it came from my imagination. When I did get a chance to research it, I found, surprisingly, that there were many cases which were similar. I then showed the script to a team of neuro-surgeons at the Alfred Hospital, fully expecting them to say it was bullshit. But quite the opposite happened. They more or less verified the feasibility and helped give the script technical authenticity. Where I had made up the names of the drugs the supplied the real names.

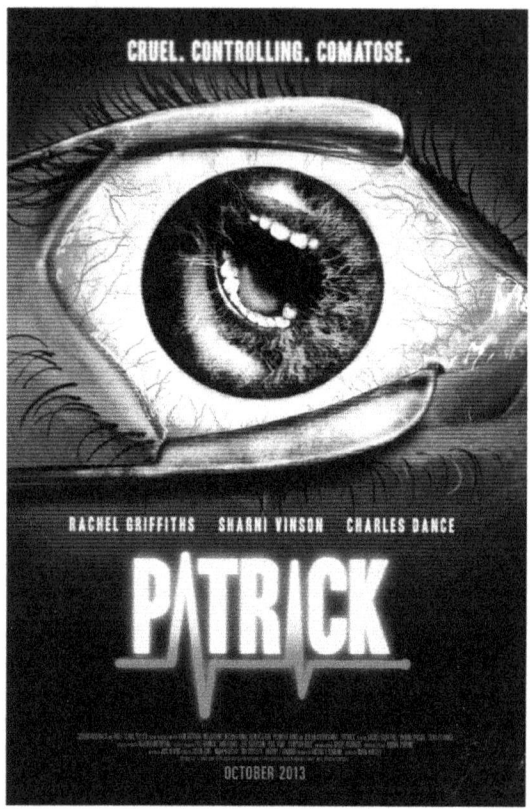

Patrick - the remake 2013

Paul Davies: The special effects in *Patrick* are quite complex. How circumscribed is a writer by what is physically practical?

Everett De Roche: Ideally, you wouldn't let it influence you, leaving such problems to the production crew. But one is inevitably conscious of such things because there is no sense writing a sequence that requires an effect you can't reproduce. At the time I conceived *Patrick* I didn't see it as a special-effects type film. But once we brought in an expert from the U.S. (Conrad Rothman), and found out what he could do, we realized how valuable special effects could be.

Paul Davies: When *Patrick* was shown during voting screenings for the Australian Film Awards in 1978 many people laughed. Did you expect that reaction?

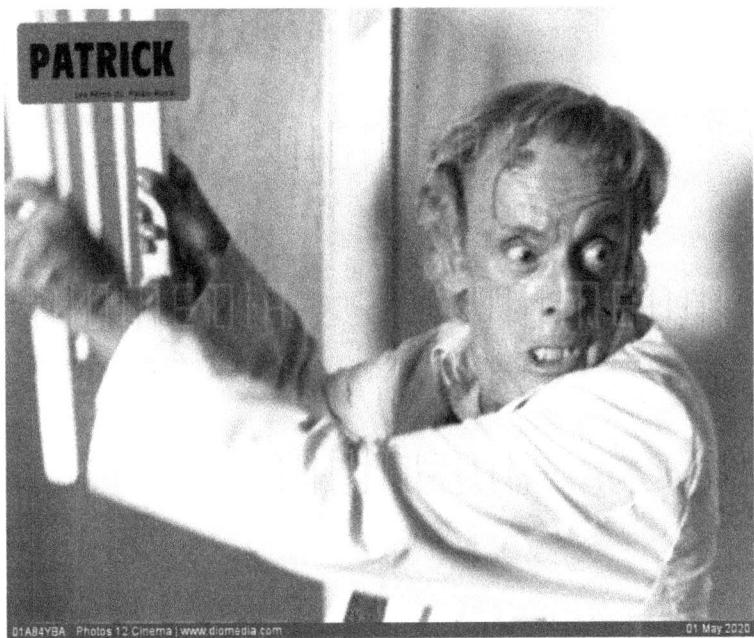

Sir Robert Helpmann as the evil Dr. Roget

Everett De Roche: We expected laughs but not necessarily in the same places. Let's face it, the Awards voters constitute and unusual audience. They have had to sit through a lot of films, some good, some bad, and *Patrick* as I remember was shown at the end. *Patrick* hasn't had that sort of reaction elsewhere. I as at a screening in Perth where people jumped where they should have jumped and laughed where they should laugh.

Paul Davies: Is *Patrick* as much a love story as a mystery-thriller?

Everett De Roche: It's a monster story, and I cut anything that didn't relate to Patrick as a monster. One of the first things to go was the romantic aspect. The biggest problem was deciding whether to make the monster the threat, or someone people would try and understand. In *Jaws,* for instance, you don't understand why the shark goes around attacking people and that's the frightening thing. Originally, I wanted to understand who Patrick was and what motivated him, but I ran the risk of it becoming boring. People just want to be thrilled.

Paul Davies: That is almost a definition of a commercial film: one that offers a thrill, instead of insight into human behaviour...

Everett De Roche: To me, commercialism is the ability to make something comprehensible to an audience. You can be subtle to the point of obscurity, which is not only bad filmmaking, but also rude. A painter can paint a picture, and if no on likes it he has only wasted his time and a bit of canvas. If you do that in films, you have wasted the money of the people who financed it, and of those who paid to be entertained.

Paul Davies: It's hard to imagine an Australian producer risking a lot on a film that was obscure…

Everett De Roche: It's a small country and no one can afford to take chances. I am talking now as if I am very commercially minded. If I were talking to a network executive, I'd take the other tack and be accused of being aesthetic and arty fartsy. The answer has to be somewhere in the middle.

Paul Davies: Is it an option to write low-budget films so that you don't have to worry as much about returns on investment?

Everett De Roche: Yes, you can write a low-budget film without compromise on quality, providing it is written with inbuilt money-savers.

Paul Davies: When did you write *Long Weekend* ?

Everett De Roche: I was writing an episode of *Bluey* and I wrote *Long Weekend* as a way of getting out of what I should have been doing. Again it was written very quickly – 10 days or so.

Paul Davies: Do you like working on several projects at once?

Everett De Roche: I don't have any choice because I can't afford to knock work back. If I have only two projects going at once I start getting worried about unemployment.

Paul Davies: *Long Weekend* is essentially a two-handed piece, though nature could be considered a third character?

Everett De Roche: Yes Nature is supposed to be the hero of the piece. The two characters, Peter and Marcia, are pretty unsympathetic. They invade the Bush and the Bush deals with them.

Paul Davies: Why do you say the Bush is supposed to be the hero?

Everett De Roche: Isn't it? Perhaps it hasn't worked. *Long Weekend* is experimental, and it relied on a number of things to work. Unfortunately the Bush comes across as a threat too early; it should have emerged as a threat after the audience had sympathized with the animals. And I don't think that sympathy is there. *Long Weekend* would have been much better if the audience had been told at the beginning that Peter and Marcia were going to die. This way, it wouldn't have had to sympathize with them, and could have concerned itself solely with when this was going to happen. Such is the nature of suspense.

Paul Davies: The ending, where Peter is killed, comes as a shock. Was there any other way of ending the film?

Everett De Roche: A large slab of the script was omitted because of the difficulty of working with animals. I wrote an enormously complicated sequence for near the end where the animals give Peter a second chance. They want him to wise up, and he is at the point of doing so when he hears a truck in the distance. He dashes off to the highway, and the animals decide there is no hope. Poetically they leave it to another man to kill him. Of course the animals can't tell you that they are the sympathetic characters; you have to rely on music, and the way things are shot. Again, unfortunately, the music in the opening sequence is very heavy, and there is a sense of menace about the animals.

Paul Davies: Are Peter and Marcia a typical Australian couple?

Everett De Roche: No. I think the film could have been set anywhere. We all go camping with the idea of getting closer to nature, armed with cans of Mortein and God knows what else. *Long Weekend* is not supposed to be a heavy environmental statement; it is just a very condensed way of saying that Nature is capable of looking after itself if man gets too out of line.

Paul Davies: Are you happier with *Patrick* or *Long Weekend* ?

Everett De Roche: I think *Patrick* was a safer story to do; it's more traditional. You know who the villain is from the start, and it develops along traditional suspense lines. *Long Weekend* is far more experimental.

Paul Davies: The characters in *Snapshot* are far less realized than those in *Patrick*. Is the difference the script or the director?

Sigrid Thornton

SNAP SHOT

M 15+ RECOMMENDED FOR MATURE AUDIENCES 15 YEARS AND OVER DVD

Everett De Roche: A lot of it has to do with the script. Richard and I worked on and off on *Patrick* for about three years, whereas *Snapshot* was written in 10 days. I think it is a great credit to Simon Wincer that he got the film off the ground.

Paul Davies: Was your working relationship with Wincer different to that with Franklin.

Everett De Roche: Yes, Richard likes to be in on every aspect of the scripting, whereas Simon prefers to look at the finished draft and act as a devil's advocate. With Simon it might be valuable to work with a script editor as well, because a writer needs someone he can ring up in the middle of the night for feedback. Simon is generally too busy to do this.

Paul Davies: Did Franklin fulfill this function on *Patrick*?

Everett De Roche: Yes. Richard and I are working on another project (*Road Games*) and even though he is on some island in Fiji, he rings me up by radio telephone every second day. He can't stand to be left out.

Paul Davies: You said that one of the things that went wrong with *Long Weekend* was that the couple is doomed. Yet *Snapshot* starts with a remarkable scene where any number of things could be happening, and up until the end one still doesn't know who is going to burn up in the room...?

Everett De Roche: The premise of a girl being pursued by a killer isn't strong enough nowadays, especially if the audience knows everything is going to turn out okay. So the idea of the flash-forward in *Snapshot* was to warn the viewer that there might not be a happy ending. This then set up an atmosphere of suspense. It was a bit of a cheat of course, because that wasn't her you saw in the beginning.

Paul Davies: Was Chris de Roche's contribution largely in the development of Angela's character?

Everett De Roche: Yes, Chris gave me a lot of feedback on how to write from a female point of view.

Paul Davies: Do you intend on working with Chris again?

Everett De Roche: I am continually using Chris as a sounding board. By giving her a credit on *Snapshot* I was acknowledging her continuing contribution. As far as other collaborations go I am working at the moment with Peter Pinny, which I am really enjoying.

Paul Davies: Is this for a feature.

Everett De Roche: No for a television series. But we are not sure what is going to happen, as it is horrendously expensive. Peter has written a number of novels, and I think he is probably the best Australian adventure writer. The novel we are adapting is based on the life of Frank Jardine who opened up the Cape York area in an attempt to turn it into another Singapore. It's a good novel but I am beginning to see the difficulties of adapting a novel to the screen. The script doesn't capture what is there in the book. That is partially because Peter writes good prose, and prose has nothing to do with scriptwriting.

Paul Davies: How did the *Harlequin* script come about?

1980	HARLEQUIN
AUSTRALIE	HARLEQUIN
FANTASTIQUE	RÉALISATEUR Simon Wincer

Everett De Roche: I wrote a treatment on spec called *The Minister's Magician*. I showed it to Simon, to Tony Ginnane and Bill Fayman, who commissioned the screenplay. It went through several drafts before everyone was happy. I then went off to Mexico and when I returned the story had been altered to remove the religious element.

Paul Davies: Why was that?

Everett De Roche: Marketing reasons. Certain overseas investors apparently had cold feet at the idea of a priest who behaves like Father Flanagan. Also the title was changed. Titles with variations on the word "magic" are a poor risk according to market research. I am told.

Paul Davies: How do you feel about alterations made by the producers?

Everett De Roche: How I feel doesn't matter. The producer pays his money, which gives him the right to use the script for dunny paper if he wants. Any scriptwriter who worries excessively about what happens to his scripts after they leave the typewriter is doomed to chronic depression. However, if alterations have to be made I would rather do them myself.

Paul Davies: Was your involvement with Wincer different from that on *Snapshot*?

Everett De Roche: Yes, very different. The story for *Snapshot* was more or less handed to us on a take-it-or-leave-it basis, whereas *Harlequin* was a story we both cared about, and wanted to do.

Paul Davies: How close is the Rasputin connection?

Everett De Roche: With the religious factor removed, there is almost no connection, which is a great pity. Religion and politics are an historically volatile duo. Czar Nicholas II would have undoubtedly given Rasputin the boot at the outset had his wife not believed him to be "a man of God". I hope audiences don't boot out Harlequin for the same reason. But certain similarities survive. Rasputin cured Alexander of haemophilia; Wolfe cures Alex of leukaemia. In the ending Wolfe's murder is an exact paraphrase of Rasputin's. After being shot several times and dumped in a river Rasputin – according to an autopsy report – in fact died of drowning.

Paul Davies: Is your interpretation of Rasputin along conventional lines, or is it based on new research: e.g. Colin Wilson's book ? (*Rasputin and the Fall of the Romanovs*)

Everett De Roche: Like most legendary figures, the myths about Rasputin have survived the truth. But I didn't set out to retell the Rasputin story. What I wanted to do was show that things have changed very little, and that a modern religious-faith healer could still accomplish what Rasputin accomplished. Yes Wilson's books were helpful.

Paul Davies: Who determined that the country in the film is unspecified, and why?

Everett De Roche: The producers, presumably on the grounds the film would appeal to a broader audience. Tony (Ginnane) and I disagree on this. Perhaps he is right – he is the authority on world markets. He is the one who has to deal with the type of mentality that insisted that *Patrick* be dubbed from English into American. I think it's absurd. But I am only the writer.

Paul Davies: Is your dialogue also non-Australian?

Everett De Roche: Yes. Again, if concessions have to be made to flog the film overseas I'd rather make them myself than leave them to some butcher in an American dubbing studio. It's ironic that for years I had to be careful not to use any Americanisms in my Crawfords scripts. Nowadays I have to substitute "windshield" for "windscreen" and "elevator" for "lift" etc.

Paul Davies: What is happening with *Yankee Zephyr*?

Everett De Roche: Richard (Franklin) is working at Columbia and is tied up with other projects. There is a first draft of the script but neither of us is satisfied with it. The script is based on the true story of an American military cargo plane (a DC3) which is reported lost while carrying the payroll for the South Pacific fleet. The plane was actually found a few years later by a pearl diver, but I have pretended it hasn't been found and that there is a race to find it. A lot of different parties are all breaking their necks to get up to Cape York, to salvage this money. At this stage we haven't decided whether it's to be a land or underwater salvage. Filming underwater presents a lot of problems unless you have a large tank. All we have is an outline and the vague idea of making it a romp in the tradition of *It's a Mad, Mad, Mad World.*

Paul Davies: Are you planning to use Cape York as the location?

Everett De Roche: It hasn't been decided. Richard and I did a reconnaissance up there a few years ago, and I am not sure it has all that much to offer which couldn't be found a lot closer to home. I was expecting dense jungle and tropical beaches, but much of it is the same as elsewhere.

Paul Davies: Is your collaboration with Franklin similar to that on *Patrick* ?

Everett De Roche: With *Patrick* there was a fairly complete draft of the script before I became associated with Richard; he then suggested improvements and changes. With *Yankee Zephyr* Richard is much more involved in the initial scripting.

Paul Davies: David Hemmings said his involvement would mean some control over its international marketability...

Everett De Roche: I believe he would be looking for a story that wouldn't depend on it being exclusively Australian – that is a story that could be told in any part of the world. The only thing Australian about the incident is that it happened here, and that Cape York is a fairly unique place because it is possible for a plane to have crashed there and remain undiscovered for 40 years.

Paul Davies: Hemmings has also said that the international market *is* the U.S. As an ex-Californian, do you feel you are uniquely placed to understand that market?

Everett De Roche: I hope so. On the whole, American films are blatantly commercial and make no bones about the fact that they are out to make money. I basically agree with that approach Film *is* a commercial medium.

Paul Davies: And with a budget of $3.5 million, one doesn't have much option.

Everett De Roche: That's right. Unless you are a Spielberg, no one is going to take lot of risks with a big budget. That would mean, I suppose, getting American leads and that sort of thing.

Paul Davies: What are your feelings about co-productions?

Everett De Roche: If they allow us to keep making films, I think it's all for the good. Certainly there should be room for completely indigenous films a well.

Paul Davies: How important is the budget to you? Do you often feel there are things you would like to have done but couldn't?

Everett De Roche: If I were given a multi-million dollar budget, I think I would know what to do with it. Usually, a writer is very aware of budgets before the script even comes off the typewriter.

Paul Davies: All your scripts are contemporary – almost aggressively so. Now you are doing a film that goes back to World War II. Is this a new direction for you ?

Everett De Roche: No because *Yankee Zephyr* is a contemporary film. The crash occurred during the war, but we are picking it up 40 years later. I have nothing against doing period films. It's just that I started writing film scripts at a time when there was a lot of period stuff around. I wanted contemporary to be different. Perhaps I also feel more comfortable with it.

Paul Davies: Is this because you can more easily relate your experience to the present?

Everett De Roche: Not really. Once I have chosen a story I then decide whether it's best told in a contemporary or period setting, and whether it's best as a feature, telefeature or episode of a television series.

Paul Davies: What are the opportunities for a writer in Australia at the moment?

Everett De Roche: There are plenty of opportunities for personal expression, even if you have to sneak it under the door. You can even say what you want in the most restricted television series.

Paul Davies: Presumably the opportunities for this would be greater in films?

Everett De Roche: That's what I thought before I got into films.

Paul Davies: Does a writer have to be self-effacing to function?

Everett De Roche: We all work differently, but a degree of self-isolation works for me. I don't like being too close to a subject, and when I am doing research I don't like anybody to know I am a writer.

Paul Davies: In *Patrick, Long Weekend* and *Snapshot* a De Roche style seems to be emerging – your obsession with water or the mystery/thriller format. Are you aware of such things?

Everett De Roche: I am, though I don't wish to be locked into any particular style. The suspense/thriller just happens to be a popular type of film at present.

Paul Davies: There is also a degree of romance and comedy in your films...

Everett De Roche: I like putting comedy into drama, but I am scared of doing straight comedy. It's hard to be funny. If you put a shock into a film, people will jump out of their seats - or they won't. And if they don't it's not a disaster. But unless you're getting laughs all the time in a comedy it's a turkey. I've never done a comedy of the Neil Simon style, but I'd love to.

Paul Davies: The comedy in *Long Weekend* is very black.

Everett De Roche: I am certainly more comfortable with black comedy. Essentially I'm a cynic.

Paul Davies: The central characters in *Patrick, Long Weekend* and *Snapshot* are all doomed to a certain extent. It is as if they have broken some moral code and are condemned. Patrick has murdered his mother; Angela seeks success at any price; Peter and Marcia are doomed because of their aggression towards the Bush. Is this part of your cynicism?

Everett De Roche: Yes. I would find it hard to create a lead character who is the typical hero or heroine; someone who behaves impeccably. I am more comfortable working with characters who have faults and pimples, who are human like the rest of us.

Paul Davies: You also concentrate on characters in the 20 to 30 age group.

Everett De Roche: I am more comfortable writing in my own age group, but there is no hard and fast rule. Sometimes I write a character who is either old, or vey young, but production or casting difficulties force me to rewrite the character in to this age group.

Paul Davies: I wondered if there wasn't something more to it. In all your films the older people prey on the younger. One thinks of Madeline in *Snapshot,* or Dr. Roget in *Patrick* ...

Everett De Roche: I am not conscious of this, and I leave it to others to figure out what it all means. Most of the time a story writes itself; I can't say I have a lot of control over it.

Paul Davies: How conscious are you of structure when writing? One of the sustaining strengths of *Patrick* for example is its manipulation of suspense...

Everett De Roche: When I did the original draft I wasn't really aware of such things, and when Richard took over, he actually charted the story. He had a scale of one to 10, and would say, "This shock is work maybe three, and the next one's five. We have a gap there, so I nee another shock. Make it worth four.

Paul Davies: Are you going through a similar process on *Yankee Zephyr*?

Everett De Roche: We are working with stunts, rather than shocks, with each stunt bigger than the last. This happens to suit the story nicely, because the closer you get to the treasure, the more difficult the terrain, the bigger the obstacles.

Paul Davies: Is it important to have a good technical knowledge, such as how shots are put together?

Everett De Roche: It can be an advantage and a handicap. It's certainly important to get out once in a while an find out what the practical difficulties are.

Paul Davies: How is it a handicap?

Everett De Roche: It may inhibit you from writing a sequence the way you want to because you're thinking that it would mean an early shoot for the crew and so on. You shouldn't think about such things; only about the story.

Paul Davies: At what stage do you show an idea to somebody else?

Everett De Roche: That is the hardest thing to decide. Do you show it at an undeveloped stage and take a chance on the director being able to understand what you're doing, or do you polish it and only give him your best shot? I tend to get anxious, and need a stamp of approval to keep going. But if someone says they don't like it, I can get discouraged and feel tempted to throw away a potentially good idea.

Paul Davies: What would your influences be as a writer?

Everett De Roche: That's a hard one because I'm not a film buff. I suppose there have been influences, but I am not aware of them. Recently I was one of the judges at a film festival, and I saw more films then than I had in my lifetime.

Paul Davies: Did it give you any perspective on Australian films in relation to global filmmaking?

Everett De Roche: My only criticism is that we are a little self-conscious at present. Ours is an adolescent industry. It's afraid of people laughing about it. It has to take more chances.

Paul Davies: Australian scripts are often criticized for being underworked. Are writers prepared to do the redrafting?

Everett De Roche: It's not a matter of not being prepared, but of not being able to afford it. If the Australian Film Commission pays $3000 for a script it gets a $3000 script. If an American studio wants a $100,000 script, then you write one. What these various producers are buying is time, and $3000 only buys a certain amount. My family and I can exist for X amount of time for $3000, and after that I can't afford to keep working on it.

Paul Davies: How important is the reaction of critics?

Everett De Roche: The things I have seen written on *Patrick* , good and bad, I have agreed with 100 per cent.

Paul Davies: Would critics make good script editors?

Everett De Roche: Not necessarily, because the critic can stand back and criticize without having to offer positive alternatives. A good script editor has to be able to criticize *and* come up with ways to improve it; not many people can do that. One thing Richard and I did on *Patrick* was to have Tom Ryan, a film critic and friend of Richard's, read the script. Tom pointed out certain things we had cheated on.

Paul Davies: In *Patrick* you appear as an electrician, and in *Snapshot* as a forensic expert. Would you like to act?

Everett De Roche: No. I like to go along for two or three days to watch the filming, but it's boring if you're not involved. The writer is the odd man out on the set, and if you are doing something, like working as an extra, you feel more a part of it.

Paul Davies: What percentage of your projects are unproduced?

Everett De Roche: Most of my failures have been television pilots. I write a lot of them – last year I did six. One guy even paid me out of his pocket because he believed in his project so much. Then it goes to a Network which says "yes" or "no" and that decision could well depend on what the executives had for breakfast. Often you feel "Jesus, if they'd only take a punt, the would see that this is going to work". There are so many things that could be done on television but aren't. It's very frustrating.

Paul Davies: Once you said the future of film-making was in television. What did you mean?

Everett De Roche: The hardest thing in film-making is to get people off their bums and into a cinema. However, the technology we now have means you no longer have to do this. If you can put a two-metre television screen into your living room and can dial a film, why would you want to pay to go to a cinema? Now this doesn't mean we won't be making films; just won't be making films for cinemas. It'll be like Home Box Office in the U.S., where people pay to see first-run films on cable television. I might be wrong, but it seems all this will increase the demand incredibly. I see less than six films a year, which is terrible for a scriptwriter, but if films were being piped into my home, I'd probably see 40. The rest of the population would do the same. The big difference this will mean in Australia is that people will have to pay to see some television shows. Up till now, television has more or less been free, as long as you put up with the ads. But people are becoming increasingly fed up with ads, and it has reached the point overseas where people are willing to pay money *not* to see them.

Paul Davies: It will obviously bring about a great many changes to television...

Everett De Roche: At the moment, television is aimed at the lowest common denominator. Dialogue has to be written so that a child can understand it, and the plots are constructed so that somebody can take a leak in the middle and not miss much. Now, if you have the selectivity of cable television, you have to win your audience. They are not just watching because you are there.

Paul Davies: What changes will this bring to the type of films we are making?

Everett De Roche: In Australian it is probably quite difficult to get money to make a film about homosexuals, draft dodgers or Aboriginals. Films have to be so broad in appeal that hopefully every man, woman, and child in the country will want to see it. But by having the selectivity of a Home Box Office situation, where you can dial whatever you want to see, it can become economically feasible to have a broad selection of material.

Paul Davies: You have also said that the television industry in Australia was healthier than in the U.S. Have you changed that view since your recent trip to the U.S.?

Everett De Roche: No. It's been confirmed even more. Australia probably has the best television in the world, and that is because we only see the best American and British shows. And the local shows – love them or leave them – have to compete with these top shows, and they usually hold their own. In the U.S. I found television, other than cable, really dull. The only exception was late night television, like *The Johnnie Carson Show* and *Saturday Night Live*. They really push comedy and good taste to the limit. I am sure there are plenty of Americans who are capable of being a lot funnier or dramatic than they are at present. It's not that they don't have creative people – after all they make some of the best films in the world – it's just that something is holding them back. I don't know what it is.

Everett de Roche (circa 2012)
"Most of it came from my imagination."

IT'S ALL IN YOUR MIND
Peter Yeldham
Cinema Papers #27 (June-July 1980)

Peter Yeldham working at home (1980)

A prolific writer for film, theatre, television and (recently) novels, Peter Yeldham's early credits include *Ride on Stranger*, *Golden Soak* and *The Timeless Land* for television plus the features, *Touch and Go* and *Weekend of Shadows*. After writing extensively for radio in Sydney, and just as television arrived in Australia (in 1956), Yeldham moved to England with his family where he remained for 20 years. With independent television taking off in the British Isles, Yeldham was employed writing for such shows as *Armchair Theatre, Shadow Squad Dial 999, Espionage, Crime Sheet, Inside Story, No Hiding Place, The Persuaders, Probation Officer, The Third Man, Van Der Valk, Zodiak, The Zoo Gang* and other British TV series. His play *Birds on the Wing*, had a long season in Berlin, and an extensive run in Paris, becoming Europe's top grossing play in 1972. More recently his books have included: *The Currency Lads* (1988) *Reprisal* (1994) *Without Warning (1995) Two Sides of a Triangle* (1996) *A Bitter Harvest* (1997) *Against the Tide* (1999) *Land of Dreams* (2002) *A Distant Shore* (2009) *Glory Girl* (2010) *The Murrumbidgee Kid* (2007) *Barbed Wire and Roses* (2008) *Above the Fold* (2014)

Peter Yeldham: When I started in radio it was a thriving industry (that was before television). However, I got a bit restless and decided to try overseas. What really got me moving away was the royal commission into the Australian television stations. I went along and heard Clive Evatt questioning Frank Packer about what he was going to do. Frank Packer refused to promise a quota, but he said "I've always treated Australians well; just trust me." So I went to Britain with my family. As expected, it was tough on my wife and our two very young children, until I actually got going.

Paul Davies: How did you get started?

Peter Yeldham: I was lucky in that I bumped into an Australian friend and he said, "Come and meet Spike Milligan." Spike had just started an agency over a fruit shop in Shepherd's Bush with a woman called Beryl Virtue, who was his agent. She also handled Simpson and Galton, Eric Sykes and Johnny Speight. Anyway, she took me on as a sort of challenge. Beryl turned out to be a marvellous agent. She soon moved into a building in Bayswater, and then into the West End. Today she is an Executive Producer for Robert Stigwood. I wrote drama plays for the first six or seven years, and then I switched to comedy, though never to the same extent as Spike and the others. They were writing situation comedy for television, which I could never do. It was a lucky meeting and Spike and the others were very good to me.

Paul Davies: So you arrived in Britain just before the golden period of British cinema.

Peter Yeldham: Yes, and just after the start of commercial television. Some pretty good things were being done for television, like *Maigret* and *Z Cars*. Unfortunately, many years later, the same things are still being done.

Paul Davies: You also wrote a number of screenplays for the major studios such as *The Liquidator* with Trevor Howard and Robert Taylor. Do you have a favourite film from that period?

Peter Yeldham: Funnily enough, it is the first one I wrote: *The Comedy Man* with Kenneth More. Although it was based on a book by Douglas Hayes about an of-out-of work actor in London, an awful lot of me went into it. I knew what it was like to be unemployed and almost starving in London. It was the most personal of the films. *The Comedy Man* was the first time I wanted to write a comedy. There is a magical moment in a crowded cinema or theatre when you hear people start to laugh; it is very heady. So, from then on, and until I came back to Australia, I was writing comedy almost exclusively, in plays and films.

Paul Davies: Everybody says Comedy is the hardest to write. What is the tip when you don't have a live audience to feed off?

Peter Yeldham: You to make yourself smile, if not laugh, when you are writing it. I have done a couple of stage plays in collaboration, and on one in particular we had the criterion that if we both laughed, the gaggle line stayed in. Sometimes, we made ourselves laugh so much that we were lying on the floor, corpsed with laughter. Occasionally though, the next day we found we had had too good a lunch and that it wasn't really that funny. It is very hard to define comedy. Of all the writers I knew, none of them were funny people. Many of them were very sad characters, forever worrying. Tony Hancock was the supreme example.

Paul Davies: Is it good to work with actors when writing comedy?

Peter Yeldham: It's usually impossible - except for stage plays. There you can work extensively with actors, particularly when you are on tour. It is quite dramatic going from town to town and you do tend to rewrite a lot. I had one play open in Liverpool called *Birds on the Wing,* which I think is the best stage play I have done. Everyone laughed all the way through. Then somebody said those terrible words, "it's going to run forever in the West End", which usually means it only runs three months. We then took the play to Coventry - where nobody laughed. It is a different humour there and the actors were far removed from the audience. It was like a different play.

Paul Davies: When things started taking off for you in Britain, did producers approach you for scripts, or were you still writing on 'spec'?

Peter Yeldham: They started coming along after the first few television shows. If you work on one television series, they'll ask you to do another one. Then somebody would see that, and ask you to do one of theirs, and so on... You get busy very quickly. I think the training I had in radio, where one had to write quickly and worked very hard, also helped. When I first went to Britain, writers felt that if they wrote something every three months they were doing a lot of work. I find that unless I am busy, I'm bored.

Paul Davies: You then came back to Australia just as the local cinema was getting off the ground...

Peter Yeldham: I returned a couple of times for visits, but I came back for good in 1976. There was a sort of déjà vu feeling about Britain in the 1970s; we just seemed to be doing the same things again. The film industry had gone pretty dead, as had television. This is one of the reasons why I came back. In fact, the only reason I stayed so long in Britain was because I was having a good run with my stage plays.

Paul Davies: Do you still have an urge to write plays?

Peter Yeldham: Yes, though I haven't written one since I came back. I find plays the hardest of all things to write in Australia.

Paul Davies: Why is that? Is it because it's easier to raise money for films?

Peter Yeldham: For a start, you have to sit down and write a play – nobody is going to ask you to write one. Also, I have been inundated with television work, and one tends to do what is paying. Another reason is that I haven't come to terms with the sort of plays I want to write out here.

Paul Davies: Looking at your record in television, one notices that you have done an extraordinary number of adaptations. Is the coincidence or have you pursued adaptations?

Peter Yeldham: Well, I hardly ever did adaptations in Britain; it was almost all originals. But since I have been back, I have worked mainly for the ABC and they like to do a lot of Australian classics. There was only one occasion where I sought out an adaptation and that was *Ride on Stranger,* which I just happened to borrow from the library one day. I intended to read a couple of chapters, but ended sitting up all night. The next day I rang Kylie Tennant and asked if the rights were still available for television. She said they were, so I went to see her. I then took out a sort of option on the book and went to the ABC with a three page outline. I also suggested they read the book, but someone replied: "No, if you're that enthusiastic, we'll do it." I think it turned out well and maybe the reason is that they put all that responsibility on me.

On location for *Ride on Stranger*
L-R Michael Aitkins, Liddy Clark, Peter Yeldham

Paul Davies: Did you have much discussion with Tennant?

Peter Yeldham: No, she stood back from it. We just had a lunch and she said, "Look, it's a book, and I know you're going to make a television series, so do exactly what you want." We made a lot of changes, but I think we kept the spirit of the book.

Paul Davies: Did you need extra research into the historical setting when adapting the book?

Peter Yeldham: No, because it was all pretty well documented in the book. Also, a lot of those things Kylie was writing about in the 1930s I had gone through in

Sydney in the late 1940s and early 1950s – the anti-communism and the Liberal fringe groups, for instance. So, again, I felt I was writing about my youth.

Paul Davies: You have also written *The Timeless Land* for the ABC. Is it a series?

Peter Yeldham: Yes. There are eight one-hour episodes. It begins in 1788 and continues for the next 22 years. It starts with Phillip, then jumps time a bit and becomes mainly concerned with the fictional characters of Eleanor Dark's book. All of this is against the authentic background of what happened – the rum trading, the revolt against Bligh and so on.

Paul Davies: Are you worried about covering some of the same historical ground as *Against the Wind*?

Peter Yeldham: Not at all. Theirs was mainly the story of a girl and her life, whereas ours is a fairly different canvas. Eleanor Dark's books were authentically researched, and we have stuck fairly carefully to history, although it is by no means a history lesson.

Paul Davies: Have you found a difference working with Australian directors as opposed to British or American ones? Is it easier to get access to a director overseas once your script has been accepted?

Peter Yeldham: Yes. When I first came back, there was a tendency to say, "Thanks for the script, now go away and we'll do it." I told them that wasn't the way I worked overseas. Luckily - working with Carl Schultz twice - I have experienced a very good working relationship. And this is now happening with other directors, as well. I just made it known that I was available at any time if they wanted to change things. I have always said, "Don't get the tea lady or the set designer to do it, call me. It's my job." I wrote this scripts of *The Timeless Land* a year ago, for example, but last week I was called in to rewrite a scene that wasn't quite right, and which was being filmed the following day. I like to follow someone through, and even be involved in, or consulted on, the editing. This happened with *The Timeless Land* and *Ride On Stranger*, and it made me feel a part of the whole thing. It wasn't the case of knocking out a script, taking the money, and going away.

Paul Davies: Another of your television shows, *Golden Soak*, starred Ray Barrett who is a personal friend. Did you have him in mind, or was that just coincidence?

Ray Barrett and David Cameron in *Golden Soak* (1979)

Peter Yeldham: Good luck really. It was a co-production, so the producers wanted somebody who would be known overseas. Ray was available, and he is known abroad and here. I was very pleased, of course. I am writing a new series for the ABC at the moment which Ray will be starring in. That has been written with him in mind.

Paul Davies: Is it an original work?

Peter Yeldham: Yes. It is called *Sporting Chance* and Ray is playing a sports journalist.

Paul Davies: When doing an adaptation, do you lift the dialogue straight out?

Peter Yeldham: Very rarely. Generally, I read the work very thoroughly twice, making notes and marking the things that are very relevant to the book. Then I can put it aside. I have absorbed so much as I want.

Paul Davies: So you don't consult it when writing?

Peter Yeldham: No. I never look at the book.

Paul Davies: Have writers ever accused you off destroying their work?

Peter Yeldham: No. The only feedback I have had was from Kylie, who wrote me a lovely letter saying she thought I had given her story a new dimension. She was very pleased.

Paul Davies: Do you think a writer should have some say in the casting?

Peter Yeldham: It is good if you can, but it's not always possible. I am usually consulted on casting, particularly when I work with Carl. We will go through *Showcast* (casting directory) together, and maybe get the choice down to three or four people. Then I leave it to him.

Paul Davies: Do you write with particular actors in mind?

Peter Yeldham: Very rarely. Once or twice I have done it and they have not been available.

Paul Davies: You have had a great deal to do with writers guilds in Australia and Britain. Do you find that writers are hard to organize industrially?

Peter Yeldham: Yes, probably because they are a very small industrial base. One of the reasons I became involved was that when I was writing radio in Australia there was no guild. We were paid and treated badly, and had no clout at all. And unless you get some kind of organization going, you will be screwed every time.

Paul Davies: Where should the main effort of the guilds be placed?

Peter Yeldham: The two main areas are our image and contracts. We recently had a long battle with the ABC over contracts, and though it was over, in another sense we were just gearing up for the next round in a few years time. We also have to put a stop to the Australian Film Commission's *50 films.* Do you realize that not one writer was mentioned? They mentioned the director, the producer, the cinematographer and the stars, but not the writer. It was quite incredible, and even a writer-producer like Joan Long was listed just as a producer. These are the things we have to stop.

Paul Davies: Do you feel there is still an ignorance of the function of writer in Australia?

Peter Yeldham: Yes, but it is certainly much better than it was. One of the amazing things that happened to me when I first went to Britain was that somebody said, "Let's talk about it over lunch." Take a writer out to lunch? Christ, that never happened to me in Australia.

Paul Davies: David Puttnam, during his recent visit, said a country could only expect to have three really great directors and four great writers. Do you think that is fair comment?

Peter Yeldham: No. It may be true of small countries like Sweden and Australia but it is certainly not true of the U.S. Actually a lot of the other things Puttnam said make sense – particularly how people always say "the trouble with Australian films is the scripts". We get some excellent scripts, some adequate scripts and some poor scripts, just like any other country. What we really lack is the creative, hustler-type Producer you find overseas. Some of them are terrible bastards to deal with, and they will screw you if they can. But if they believe in your work, they will fight to the death to get it produced. Whereas in Australia, with all the insecurity at present one only needs to get frown from the AFC commissioner before somebody says "Let's change the script." We had this problem with the one real disaster I wrote here, *Weekend of Shadows*. We had a constant changes and insecurity about it, right up to the day of shooting. I think many of these changes didn't help the film.

Poster for *Weekend of Shadows* starring John Waters (1978)

Paul Davies: There is a lot of discussion about ensuring our films are more international in flavour. Having worked here and abroad, what do you see as the necessary ingredients?

Peter Yeldham: It is hard to answer. But the best way to be international is to be truly national. If you go for a mid-Atlantic or a mid Pacific type product, that's what you end up with. It probably plays to packed houses in Fiji, but that's all. The British found this in film and television. It was only when they started making genuinely British shows that they started selling overseas. In some ways it is like the situation with *The Sullivans*: it is a very Australian show, yet it is starting to sell in the U.S.

Paul Davies: You were in Britain during the recent rise and fall of the film industry. Do you see any common trends in Australia?

Peter Yeldham: The failure rate is growing, as we make more films. That first honeymoon, when people went to see Australian films because they were Australian, is over. And what is happening in its place is this tendency to say "We have to sell to the U.S. so let's Americanise it. That's what worries me most of all, because it may mean we become a service industry like the British.

Paul Davies: Do we have a screenwriting industry in Australia?

Peter Yeldham: If you include television, it is becoming quite an industry. I am not sure but there must be about 25 Half hours of serials a week and that means quite a few writers are employed. How long they work on those series is, of course, another thing. Even in the best days in Britain people used to say that most of the writing was being done by about 50 writers even though there were 800 members in the British guild. I guess it is somewhat the same here.

Paul Davies: Rosemary Anne Sisson remarked two years ago that she was amazed to find that there were so many active professional writers in Australia. Are we the lucky country in that respect?

Peter Yeldham: I hope we're going to be a lucky country, and it is a battle that will keep going on. We're always in danger of television stations cutting out and films failing, though at the moment we're doing alright. I think a good sign is the shorter series which the commercial stations are doing. Hopefully out of those will come some quality shows which we can sell abroad.

Paul Davies: Do you see the shorter series as a reaction against the endlessness of the serials?

Peter Yeldham: I think so. Some of those serials do go on and on. Still, the advantage of the serial is that people are working, and you can only get better by working. We have a good depth of acting talent; what we need is a lot more directors and writers. But the situation is improving all the time.

Paul Davies: Could you tell us about your new film *Touch and Go*?

Chantal Contouri, Wendy Hughes, Carmen Duncan
Touch and Go (1980)

Peter Yeldham: It is a light and entertaining comedy-thriller. The original idea was Peter Maxwell's, who is the director. The idea was to use Hayman Island and, because of Reg Ansett's connection with the place, and Ansett Airlines. But Ansett could never see the joke about having this island robbed. We should've known, I suppose, after looking at his photograph.

Paul Davies: You haven't refloated the idea with Rupert Murdoch?

Peter Yeldham: No. By that time we had the money together.

Paul Davies: What's the hardest part about writing?

Peter Yeldham: Starting. The first five or so pages often takes me days. I once did a stage play and the first act took me three months, while the second took six days. I suppose it's all in your mind, but I always find the second half of the script is written much more quickly than the first.

Paul Davies: There is a great emphasis these days on having a script editor. How important are they?

Peter Yeldham: I find an editor can be handy, but I preferred to work with the director, or even the executive producer. The advantage of the script editor is, if you get stuck in the middle, you can ring him up and have him throw ideas at you. On the whole, though, the function of the script editor should be as unobtrusive as possible.

Paul Davies: Can you imagine going back to work in Britain?

Peter Yeldham: No, I think my future is here. I have really enjoyed these past couple of years. When I first left Australia, people thought a scriptwriter was the man who sat in the back of a chemist shop, copper plating the bottles of old medicine. At least now, when you say you are a writer, they don't ask "But what do you do for a living?" That is the big improvement since I left.

Paul Davies: You are part of a generation of Australians who left this country out of the belief that there weren't big opportunities here...

Peter Yeldham: Yes. Quite apart from what I said about Frank Packer, I really went abroad for a year or two to get some experience, which a lot of other people did. But it went so well for me that I stayed. Actually, a lot of people still can't quite forgive me for being away all that time. "Expatriate" has become a sort of dirty word. When I grew up, expatriates were glamorous figures, like Ernest Hemingway and F. Scott Fitzgerald. But in Australia it became: "You abandoned us."

Paul Davies: You have a number of future plans, but do you have an overall strategy?

I have this new series for the ABC, which is going to take me all year, and I have a couple of ideas for films which I would like to do. I'd also like to work again as a writer and co-producer, as I did on *Touch And Go*, because I really enjoyed being involved in pre-and post-production.

Paul Davies: Very few writers are in that position...

Peter Yeldham: Yes, and more of us should be. I know Joan Long and Margaret Kelly are trying to do this, as is John Dingwell. Obviously, we need experience producers beside us, but giving writers are creative say Will help our films and help us as well.

"the best way to be international is to be truly national"

Peter Yeldham
Filmography

AUSTRALIA
<u>Features</u>
Touch and Go
Weekend of Shadows

<u>Television Series</u>
Ride on Stranger
Run from the Morning
Golden Soak
The Timeless Land

<u>Television Play</u>
Money in the Bank

BRITAIN

<u>Features</u>
The Comedy Man
The Liquidator
The Long Duel
Age of Consent
Our Man in Marrakesh
10 Little Indians
24 hours to Kill

<u>*Stage Plays*</u>
Birds on the wing
Fringe benefits
But She Won't Lie Down
Away Match

<u>Television Plays</u>
Thunder on the Snowy
A Visit from Anna
East of Christmas
The Cabbage Tree Hat Boys
A Sort of Stranger
The Gambler
A Dragon to Kill
Reunion Day
The Juggler
A Really Good Jazz Piano
Ant and the Grasshopper

Co-Produced Television Series
Birds on the Wing
The Five Midnights
Mis-adventure
Harriet's Back in Town

Television Series
Love Story
Maigret
No Hiding Place
Van der Valk
The Zoo Gang (U.S. series)
Espionage (U.S. series)
The Persuaders
Ward 10
Probation officer
Zodiac
The nurses (U.S. series)
The Third Man

Helen Mirren, James Mason *Age Of Consent* (1969)

In recent years Peter Yeldham has turned to writing novels with some of his most popular recent works being:

A Bitter Harvest
Barbed Wire and Roses
The Last Double Sunrise
Beginning with an Empty Page
The Murrumbidgee Kid

From screenwriter to book author

MAKING THE FICTUMENTARY
Paul Davies
Cantrills Filmnotes #35/36 (April 1980)

EXITS was written by Paul Davies who produced and co-directed it with Pat Laughren and Carolyn Howard. The film includes poems by Eric Beach (*No No No* and *Mr. Fraser's Car*) plus music by Ken Schroeder. It was a no-budget short feature made with a small grant for post-production from the Australian Film Commission. *EXITS* was a finalist in the Greater Union Awards at the 1980 Sydney Film Festival and was also invited to the Melbourne Film Festival the same year. It premiered as one of the last events to go on at Melbourne's iconic Pram Factory theatre on 11/11/1980; screening alongside John Hughes' experimental video *NOVEMBER 11* and an exhibition of paintings relating to "The Dismissal" by Antonio Muratore.

Painting of Gough Whitlam used in the film by Wayne Larsen
Crew:
Camera: Paul Cavell,
Sound: Lynton McFadzean
Editing: Rob Scott
47 minutes, Colour and B&W (Melbourne 1980)

CAST

Caz Howard (Anna)

Paul Davies (George)

Mary Anne Grey
(Rose)

Robert Antoniades
(The Manager)

Charlie Dale (The Digger)

"We set out to make a feature for the cost of the film stock and the hire of a camera
and sound recorder. It wasn't just 'low budget' it was '*no* budget'"
Paul Davies – The First Australian History and Film Conference,
National Library, Canberra, November 1981

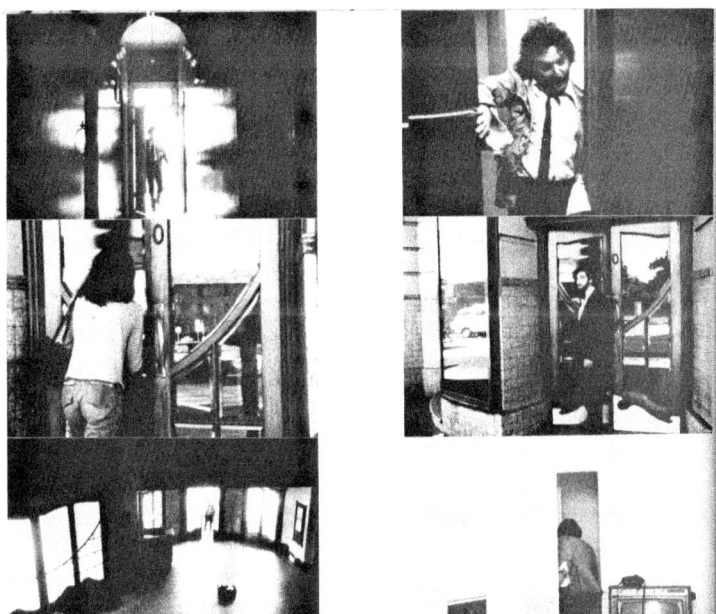

Entrances and Exits in *Exits*

What is the relationship between the media and politics? To what extent does one control the other, and how can we assess that control? The most obvious point is that people who own or work in the media exert enormous influence on society. Conversely, most people - the vast majority - have no influence on public events; on events which for better or worse shape their lives. *Exits* is a look at that world from their position, an historical narrative dealing with the events of November 11 1975, the day on which the Labour government of Gough Whitlam was removed from office. The film examiners the effect of this dramatic change of power on a handful of characters wandering around Melbourne: ordinary people trapped by extraordinary circumstances.

And yet contained within Malcolm Fraser's grab for power is a stark revelation of the flimsy constitutional base on which all parliamentary authority rests. Australia has always been, and still is essentially, a monarchy. The most powerful figure in the land is someone called the Governor General who also just happens to be the Commander-in-Chief of the Armed Forces. The irony is that it all happened on Remembrance Day: the 11th hour of the 11th day of the 11th month. The moment at which people commemorate the terrible slaughter of the First World War. As the official propaganda of the day would have it, this was the "war to end all wars."

Irony became a key factor in organizing the historical material for the film. A reflection on the actual course of events provided a simple "documentary" structure on which we could hang the growing bewilderment and outrage of the "fictional" characters whose viewpoint the film takes.

November 11, 1975 – A CHRONOLOGY

Pre-9 am. Newspaper headlines promise a "way out" of the 10 week old constitutional crisis brought on by the Senate's refusal to pass the Budget. Gough Whitlam and Malcolm Fraser, we were told, are at last going to sit down and talk.

9.00 am The meeting lasts three-quarters of an hour and solves nothing.

10.30 am Whitlam tells Caucus there are enough funds for a half senate election.

11.45 am The house of Representatives sits and a no-confidence motion in the government is turned into a no confidence motion in Malcolm Fraser.

12.40 am Whitlam leaves Parliament House for "Yarralumla", the Governor General's residence, to advise a Half-Senate election. He has spoken to Kerr about this earlier and receives the impression that the Governor General has no objection.

12.45 am Malcolm Fraser arrives at Yarralumla ahead of Whitlam and is ushered into a side room while his driver is told to park the car around the back.

1.00 pm Whitlam arrives and is immediately sacked by Kerr.

1.30 pm Fraser is sworn in as the caretaker Prime Minister and returns to the Liberal Party meeting in Parliament House to announce that he is the only legal Federal Minister.

2.25 pm The Senate passes the budget.

2.28 pm The House of Representatives passes a motion of no confidence in Fraser.

2.42 pm Fraser tries unsuccessfully to adjourn the House.

3.00 pm The House of Representatives orders the Speaker, Gordon Scholes, to see the Governor General and advise him to recommission Mr. Whitlam.

4.30 pm Scholes arrives and is told an appointment has been made for 4.45pm.

4.45 pm The Governor General's secretary David Smith reads the proclamation dissolving parliament to an angry crowd of students and public servants.

David Smith reads the proclamation dissolving Parliament

Spontaneous demonstrations occurred throughout Australia. 10,000 people gathered in Melbourne's city Square and later marched on to Government House, the Liberal Party headquarters in South Melbourne, and to the Robert Menzies' Centre in Albert Road. The following day in Sydney a group of people smashed through a police line and charged into the Stock Exchange. Four and a half weeks later Malcolm Fraser was elected to power with the largest majority in Australian history.

Out of consideration for these events was born the desire to make a film about the influence of political changes on the fortunes of ordinary people. It seemed that people always got closest to the truth when caught in an exaggerated situation. *Exits* was inspired by the Whitlam sacking and written on scraps of paper in the streets, trams, and lane ways of Melbourne over a 12 month period in bits and pieces at nights and weekends. Most of the documentary material, the press conferences, the demonstration footage and the idea for the subtitles was incorporated into the film after the principal shooting of the basic story had been completed.

There was never any grand plan. It seemed to us, simply, that 16mm film-making was a more accessible form of expression than most people were prepared to admit. We had enough money to buy the film stock and rent a Nagra (tape recorder) and a crystal-sync camera (an Arriflex 16mm). The intention then was to "locate" the film back in the streets and the public transport on which it was conceived. The context (the background of the streets, the dump, the pub and the cinema) was vital in supplying a certain documentary validity to the "invented" story of the characters - particularly so if this was two intercut with actual press conferences and media reports of the time.

Above all we wanted to make a film about escape and to do so in such away that the boundaries between recorded fact and constructive fiction were always floating. In this way people might see that the emotional reaction of the characters, their assessment of the political events, is more valid then the dry language of the media. It follows that if Australia was still rooted in a political system devised in 19th Century England, then the whole place is still, as it then was, a kind of prison. The Whitlam years must now be seen as a failed attempt to break out of our colonial situation. That at least is the macro view. On the micro level people colonise each other.

Against the larger exits of Whitlam from power, Anna from Melbourne, and the "Digger" from life are set the minute by minute escapes that everybody makes when the room or the other people in it have become intolerable. Anna, the cinema usher quits her job, and a little later is again walking out on her former manager in the pub. The film opens with George coming out of the building where he works, at a loss as to what to do with the rest of the day. He wanders aimlessly around town, buying papers, and finally settles on the cinema, which is itself another exit from reality.

Here he meets Anna and later, as the news of Whitlam's sacking comes through, Anna and George try to rationalize the significance of it all. In the absence of any real access to the facts our characters have no option but to react on a level of paranoia, or on a level of individual retaliatory action which is doomed to politically. For this reason, George reads a conspiracy theory into the crossword puzzle of that morning's newspaper. His first words in the film as he gets into a lift are "we theorize within the sound of guns", a rough definition of the plight of the Australian intellectual and a prophetic clue as to the true nature of the day's events - recalling again, that the Governor General is both the military and political head of government.

"Remembrance Day" Collage

Shortly after at 11 am the guns fire symbolically at the Shrine of Remembrance. And from then on military images recur. Later in the pub George tells Anna that "starting a war or changing a government" are basically the same thing. The intention in both cases is essentially the same. To overturn the existing social and political order.

The war images accumulate around the character of the Digger a fading personality wrecked by alcohol. He alone seems to take the ceremony of Remembrance Day seriously. And yet his exit, his only option for a way out, is to hang himself (thus meeting a fate handed out to Ned Kelly by British justice on the 11th of November 1880). Remembrance Day = Religion + War.

As the film progresses through the morning and on into the afternoon of November 11, the established media legitimize social upheaval through a process of dealing "objectively" only with the superficial facts (the world of the press release) at the expense of the underlying causes of events: the subjective motives of class interest, political and national self-interest.

Exits attempts to supply this missing aspect of the causes of the coup by presenting the case of the five characters: a cinema manager, the two ushers who work for him (including Anna), the Digger and George. In this way a fictional/emotional account is pitted against the so-called real account; personal history grapples with the media record and their relative validity is left in the hands of the audience.

Only Anna seems to take a strongly individualistic course. She is best able to come to terms with the personal consequences of political and social alienation in her story about the young man who bails up a family in her street with a bush knife. This is in fact a real story, based on an event that once occurred in my street. The pent up fury and random violence of that young man against all authority seemed symptomatic of the feelings many people shared towards the events of Remembrance Day 1975. Anna's position, broadly, is that the whole thing is personal: politicians, to her, act out only the charade of power. Without parliament things would continue much as they always have done. George, on the other hand, is locked in a more class-oriented view of society. He can find no way out at all. At the end of the film he returns to his room to find it evacuated. Everything has been taken. No reasons are supplied. It's just all gone. The film opens in this room with Whitlam on the radio assuring us that the causes of the Labour Governments' problems are external. It ends with the voice and image of Fraser assuring us that "we'll all get used to the change".

The film starts out in the manner of a traditional narrative drama. We see the characters waking up on November 11 and going to work. Subtitles establish the date, and some quick inter-cuts of Whitlam and Fraser arriving at Parliament House establish the format. Thereafter the fortunes of the characters and the politicians parallel each other. Anna is sacked at the moment that Whitlam is, and from then on the cinema where she works "The National Theatre" (like the 29th Parliament) starts to fall apart.

But cutting through all this are the poems and the music. At certain key points the narrative is abandoned in favour of war imagery, a collage of press conference statements from Fraser, or a poem. The effect is cumulative rather than linear. The film, through the poems, attempts to supply a context that the media constantly censors. Eric Beach's poems also remind us that behind all the contortions of what actually happens is the issue of who rules and who loses, i.e. the issue of class:

NO NO NO

Work all day got nothin t' show
They sweat my pay, just another Joe Father Xmas,
ho ho ho
No no no
No no no
This can't be the place where the Liber-als go

Some got pull
Some got shoelaces
Turn on the lights, how come I still can't see their faces?
Lots of dough
No no no
No no no
This can't be the place where the Liber-als go.
I brought you a tram ticket, oh
Some Jaffas to rattle at the show
Father Xmas ho ho ho
No no no
No no no
This can't be the place whether Liber-als go.

Eric Beach

The poems have this summing-up quality about them. They condense the focus of the film to the key issues: class, power, alienation, and behind all of them: war. The visual images amplify the poetic metaphor and enforce the rhythm. The last poem therefore becomes a summary of the whole day:

MR. FRASER'S CAR IS JUST AROUND THE CORNER, RAG

Gough was first, but he was last,
Shake it when the Queen goes past
Big black car, my big black past
Goes to show the Queen has class
All you loyal subjects take your hat off to me
Cause I'm so square
Cause I'm so rare
Get your Xmas message here.

I don't want no Melbourne club
Silverware now there's the rub

Turn your glass down at the pub
Guff is Gough has lost his job
All your little people take your hat off to me
Cause I'm rag
Cause I'm a rag
Cause I'm a rag-time millionaire

Discount store has got my pay
Discount I still work all day
Discount what the papers say
Discount when the cow make hay
All you little people take your head off to me
Cause I'm so hmmm…
Cause I'm so aaah…
Cause I'm so la de da de da.

Western District we're are all friends
VW loves Mercedes-Benz
Means have gone beyond our ends
Got the economic bends
All you little people take your head off to me
Cause I'm no fool
I pulled the wool
I'm a full time millionaire

Vote for me on coup d'état
Genuinely needy – ta
If my diction seems contra
Tell the ABC it's war
All you little people take your head off to me
Cause I'll go far
Cause I'll go far
I'm round the corner in the car.

                                                            Eric Beach

"You'll get used to the change" Malcolm Fraser
Post-coup press conference, November 11, 1975

Contained within the events of November 11 1975 is a great deal of what can only be described as farcical. This is not to take away from the seriousness of what happened. But plainly much of it was absurd, ludicrous. There are sequences in *Exits* which match this, which don't appear to make any sense: George walks past a yellow cab sitting empty in the street with one door open and the radio on. He reaches in through the passenger side and pulls out two Billy Graham pamphlets, stares at them and walks onto the pub. On the cab radio we hear the morning news bulletin assuring us that there is going to be a half-Senate election after all. Whitlam appears to have survived the crisis brought on by the denial of Supply.

But the Billy Graham pamphlets are the disturbing note. Whenever religion comes into it there's bound to be deception. The morning news, like the headline "Hope For Way Out – Leaders Meet Today", lulls us into a false sense of security.

Shortly afterwards George discovers an abandoned *Herald* in the pub announcing Whitlam's dismissal, and Kerr-ist ! The nightmare has begun. The film is immediately interrupted buy a newsflash and quick series of handheld shots in the streets, nervous, jerky, point-of-view images with the newsreader's voice cut across two tracks to give an ominous "Big Brother-ish" effect. We hear George's voice raving to an unseen cab driver and laid over this, another media account of the sacking. But by now all accounts sound the same, because in effect they are reading off the same press release, the one put out by Fraser and Kerr. Sound and picture build to a climax with George yelling in the street, urging total strangers to fight back. But even in his lonely gestures there is the all pervading sense of failure, paranoia, doom. As Anna says to him later: "it's all too late. You're too late."

She is the only character with a direct solution. She goes home, packs her bag, and delineates her reasons for leaving (exiting), front-on to the camera: "the farce is over," - only to return to the pub again, and after that the cinema. Finally, she goes off on a tram outside Luna Park.

The Cinema Manager (who remains nameless) is given some money by Rose (Mary Anne Grey -the other usher). He puts some of it on a horse and gives the rest to Anna, who promptly gives it back to Rose, thus exposing the manager's deception. Favouring one employee above the other, ripping off Rose essentially.

But what looks like a plot becomes merely a series of circular gestures. Money, politics, power goes round and round. Meanwhile the characters in *Exits* are all trapped, all prisoners either consciously or unconsciously of factors outside their control. The Governor General sacks Whitlam as Prime Minister and appoints Malcolm Fraser as the new Prime Minister. When Fraser goes back to Parliament and immediately loses the confidence of the House, the Governor General dissolves in it, ignoring the call of the Speaker for him to reappoint Whitlam. Somehow, in all this there is something peculiarly Australian. The muddle and the hopelessness. No kind of a truly genuine social progress seems possible.

A first assembly of the film was about two hours long. The key decision in cutting it to 50 minutes was the abandonment of anything that went against the idea that here we have five fairly ordinary characters, living out fairly ordinary, unexciting lives, yet passing through the most traumatic political circumstances. We wanted to have the option of telling the truth (all the documents, references, telexes, and a lot of the dialogue are based on fact) with the higher appropriateness of dramatic licence. That licence though, had to contain the core of the certain a emotional validity, otherwise we ourselves would be party to a general deception. Again, how successfully this works depends on the audience.

When friends heard about our work and the collective nature of it, documentary footage, music, poems, books, telexes, clues, began to flow in. as we assimilated this material into the body of the film it soon became obvious that there was no need to invent a plot. The "plot" was the events of the day itself.

To make the whole thing work with the limited resources available we had to complete the shoot in 10 days with the crew of four people. We chose the fast reversal stocks largely created for television news gathering and prepared a fairly detailed shooting script. Again the idea was to transfer the documentary technique to narrative drama. The theory worked a lot better as the shoot progressed. Towards the end we were doing scenes in one take, improvising dialogue and keeping the camera moving as much as possible. The fast stocks allowed us to do most of this without any additional lighting. This saved time and made the one-shot, one-take strategy possible: the Luna Park scene, the beach scene, the crossword scene in the pub, and the scene in the cab at night are all examples of this.

There was never anybody really in charge of the film. No "auteur" as such. . To a certain extent Pat Laughren and I worked out the angles and blocked scenes the night before each day's shoot – this helped, and it gave us the feeling that we knew what we were doing, but it didn't necessarily dictate how things had to be done. Likewise, the boundaries between cast and crew were pretty fluid. All the crew, at some stage, appear in film. Pat, Carolyn Howard, Rob Scott and I were responsible for the cutting. At various stages we'd screen the work in progress for others who had worked on the film and their reactions influenced any further cutting that followed.

After the broad structure of the film had been laid down, it's bore little resemblance to the original script, especially as we developed the idea of cutting from the general (media account) to the particular (fictional narrative). Having set up a sequence in this way the key question then was "Does this work?" If there wasn't an immediate consensus we'd fiddle with it until it seemed right. Only towards the end of the fine cut, when things had to be truly fixed, did this process of consensus-editing become difficult.

The attempt was above all to capture the shock people experience when they've been lulled into a full sense of security about the world and how they react when they discover (uncomfortably) something (life, politics, history) will never be the same again... or will it? ... or is it?

In History all things occur twice
Once as tragedy, once as farce:
Chile September 11, 1973
Australia November 11, 1975

A THREE-DIMENSIONAL IMAGE DANCING IN FRONT OF YOU
Keith Thompson
Cinema Papers # 34 (September-October 1981)

Keith Thompson at the Australian Film and Television School 1981

After the early success of some of his work with the BBC, Keith Thompson came to Australia in the early 1970s to work at Crawford Productions on the last few episodes of the long running *Homicide* series. This included a special 90 minute episode called *Stopover* which won him the AWGIE and SAMMY awards for 1976. Later at the ABC, he originated the *Truckies* series and produced his most highly acclaimed work *Gail,* the story of a young girl's struggle with her family. Since then he has been working on a number of feature scripts and was appointed to the AFTS in mid-1980 a year before this interview took place.

The Australian Film and Television School

As the needs and commitments of writers tend to vary a great deal, the Australian film and Television School in Sydney offers a range of courses in writing for the screen. There is the original one-year course for writers of certain "proven" ability. This involves a six month technical orientation in film production and a six-month residency, working closely with the Full Time Program, supplying material which is then produced on film or tape by student directors. In 1982, it is hoped there will also be a full three-year course, so that script writing will, like camera, sound, editing and production management, be a major course of study within the AFTS.

Operating for the first time this year, and supported by the Literature Board of the Australia Council for the Arts, is a three to four month crash course in scriptwriting designed for established novelists, playwrights, journalists and poets. The cross-fertilization of novel-writing or play-writing with writing for the screen is seen as an exciting one. What the AFTS is looking for here, apart from quality of ideas, is a certain kind of visual consciousness.

According to Keith Thompson, newly appointed head of the Writing Workshop, Australian filmmakers can't, or don't talk about films in a very creative way. He sees the writer as the spearhead through the prevailing low standard of television drama. Until now, writers have copped the flak, but what is more at fault is some sort of general conception of what filmmaking actually is – or can be. Thompson wants to "exploit" the notion of what scriptwriting can deliver – from the writer's point of view and for the industry at large. He sees the AFTS as the place where the debate must begin.

Thompson describes the AFTS as a "crucial resource", one to be exploited by not just the writers enrolled there, but also by people outside the school. He has developed the notion of the Writing Workshop at 10 Lyonpark Rd, North Ryde, as a drop-in centre. A number of open seminars are being organized - a kind of "mini-writing festival" with papers from people like Everett de Roche (*Patrick*), Howard Griffiths (ABC), Tony Morphett (*The Sullivans*) and British screenwriter Barry Took (*Monty Python*).

The intention is to keep things as free form as possible. At the very least, it is a place where one can find writers at work; at best, and in concert with organisations like the Writers Guild, it is a place where one can get a second opinion on a script; even a place where you can find actors ready to read a script and perhaps put bits of it on tape.

This aspect of the Writing Workshop fits in with the general aspirations of the Open Program of the AFTS, but Thompson and Austin Steele (writing consultant to the Open Program) also see the drop-in centre as recruitment for the major courses. Steele, in conjunction with the South Australian Film Corporation, has been running workshops in Adelaide and it is hoped to extend these activities to Melbourne, Brisbane and Perth.

As a by-product of his teaching function, Thompson is keen to isolate three major film styles or languages and to examine their influence on what might be seen to be an Australian film style. Firstly there is the British film language: a kind of documentary/realist tradition rooted somewhere in the Puritan work ethic and a style that best accounts for Britain's success with television. The British docu-drama, Thompson feels, is perfectly suited to the sort of naturalistic medium that sits in a corner of one's living room. Secondly, there is the American film style: the traditional three act play structure. And finally, a European style: the first person, singular film.

Of course this is by no means an exhaustive list, but it is felt these are the dominant influences on Australia's tradition. The danger for Thompson is that the influences operate in Australian work rather haphazardly. When one doesn't know where the influences are coming from, the result is a bit of a mess – first person, singular films say, operating in a dramatized documentary.

Paul Davies: Have you come to any early conclusions about a separate Australian tradition actually emerging?

Keith Thompson: There is probably some kind of synthesis of European, American and British traditions. But the odd thing is you can't actually relate Australian literature to Australian films, as you can say, with the British cinema. You just can't relate the bush ballad and that historical experience to the urban landscape; that narrative breaks down in the city. A key component of American films has always been the possibility of movement through a society or through a landscape. These are two movements around which you can build a firm structure. In Australia we have explored landscape in a photographic sense, but not movement *through* a landscape – and we have an ideal country to explore this, with shifts of migration and so on. The problem with the British dramatized documentary is that, because it comes out of the puritan work ethic culture, from Cromwell onwards, you can't allow yourself the freedom to dramatize. It is austere, without decoration, and enormously concerned with reality. It is as if the whole British psyche won't allow that flowering unless it is first rooted in realism. The most advanced British work, if you like, is still expressionist documentary: *Rock Follies* and *The Naked Civil Servant. Pennies From Heaven* is another good example because although it is rooted in naturalism it is looking to flower.

Paul Davies: It does have the element of the fantastic about it: the sudden bursting into song in the bank manager's office and so on...

Keith Thompson: Yes. Whereas in Spanish cinema say, even in an ordinary cops and robbers thriller there are overtones of surrealism, which is ritual and Catholic. The British tradition is inherent through their literature. There is a line connecting their television and their literature, which isn't there in Australia – it is broken.

Paul Davies: What about the connection between the playwriting of the early 1970s and the consequent surge in Australian filmmaking?

Keith Thompson: Perhaps, I wasn't here in the early 1970s, so I am not quite sure. It is very difficult to say just where the Australian industry is heading now.

Paul Davies: But here, in the Australian Film and Television school you are in a key position to influence that direction...

Keith Thompson: The School is, as a whole, conscious of this. I would say it has a commitment to exploring the Australian contemporary lifestyle.

Paul Davies: Does that tend to put it in the British mould of documentary realism?

Keith Thompson: I wouldn't like to limit it to that extent. What the School, and certainly the Writing Workshop, should be doing is seeing where the individual interests of the students lie, and working towards those interests. We have to develop skills and push them to the limit – although that probably just reflects my puritan work ethic.

Paul Davies: But it's also economic isn't it? It is easier to make a contemporary film set in the streets than an historical epic...

Keith Thompson: I have a perception of the Australian industry – of which I am a part; I am not saying that as a migrant – as being distanced from the emotional content. It holds emotional content at arms length. In fact it holds most issues at arms length. That's partly reflected in the emphasis on historical features. I also wonder about the odd predilection of most Australian male writers, myself included, to write about women. That is a way of not writing about themselves directly. It is a device men have of getting women to carry their emotional content. To that extent it is a cop-out.

Paul Davies: But I would have thought *Gail* was an example of the reverse. You used an inversion of personalities – yours into hers – to come up with a particularly credible character.

Keith Thompson: It is interesting because it got below people's belts and that's what I think plays should do. I showed it to school teachers – psyche and guidance people – and they wouldn't talk about the play, they would talk about "I". They'd see themselves in it. That emotional response is what I am looking for, and I don't know how much that just reflects what I am. I don't like the distance writers and directors put between themselves and their material. One of the advantages of a place like the AFTS is that you can explore on two levels: you can explore the "out there", the contemporary lifestyle, and you can bring the material home and explore it within yourself. That's why it is an AFTS priority to get out into the real world, research and look at the contemporary Australian life, and bring student consciousness to bear on that. The two things have to mould, somehow. It is also part of the general "seeing if there is an Australian film language – the "critical" function of the School.

It is interesting being British and being brought up in that documentary realist tradition. I was 18 when *Cathy Come Home* went on television. I'd seen some of the Ken Loach things that preceded it. I realized I used the standard drama that the British incorporate into their films – shots of people walking in the streets, so that you think you are in a realistic setting. I had done that unconsciously for years, because that's where I come from. But when I came here, I don't know what tradition to put myself into; I didn't feel like I was on any kind of river. In Australia you have to start from scratch; you have to discover the Australian style for yourself. Maybe, as writers, we are just too close to the Australian industry to see if it has a voice.

Paul Davies: Is this the fault of the critics? Perhaps the Australian media hasn't provided a sufficient analysis of its own work?

Keith Thompson: I feel quite strongly that there is no critical establishment – certainly in television. There are some exceptions, though, like the stuff 3RRR puts out – John Flaus and so on.

Paul Davies: So the best analysis comes from the academics and not the media...

Keith Thompson: Yes, with one or two exceptions like Brian Courtis (*The Age*). There isn't, as a rule, any debate about television – not by anyone who understands television. But, generally, the criticism that is around just isn't working to the benefit of the film or television program maker. It is working on an academic level, within the colleges; that's why it is vital that we incorporate it as an aspect of the AFTS. But it isn't working on a craft/criticism level, or even a gut level, which the best overseas criticism does.

Paul Davies: Does the School have the chance to develop new formal possibilities with film and television, or is there a counter-pressure to merely provide a training facility for the industry?

Keith Thompson: There is certainly that pressure at the moment, with the tax incentives (10 BA), but again it is a matter of responding to people who come into the School. There are those who come to acquire craft skills and don't avail themselves of the chance to do direction. They are just here to polish skills. In that sense, the School is very successful. For example, there is a 100 per cent employment rate out of the sound workshop.

Paul Davies: Is that a consequence of the present economic climate?

Keith Thompson: I think it has always been like that.

Paul Davies: How about Camera and Writing?

Keith Thompson: There has been about a dozen people through the Writing Workshop, and as far as I know, they are all working in the industry. Steve Wallace did the one year course; Rifka Hartman and Patricia Johnston were in the same year. And the three people from last year are all writing features.

Paul Davies: How many people apply for the courses? It must be hard settling for only three or four for each (three-month, one year, three year) course...

Keith Thompson: There is about a one in 30 or 40 chance of getting in. But, like creative development submissions the good ones leap out at you.

Paul Davies: But an almost guaranteed job at the end of it?

Keith Thompson: I suppose you could say guaranteed job if not funding...

Paul Davies: Surely it is also the chance to make a film here that is so attractive?

Keith Thompson: I have tried to re-emphasize what the Writing Unit should be about. It used to be a three week technical orientation with an 11 month residency. I have tried to balance that out, so that it is half and half. I think it is unrealistic to expect to take writers out of their prime working circumstances, established over a number of years, bring them into those four offices down the corridor and expect them, no matter what creative input they are getting from the rest of the School, to suddenly come up with the major work of their lives. It is more important that they come here, absorb everything around the place, do some writing – it is important that they write something – and then go away and let this place react on them over the next eight or ten years. – whatever.

Paul Davies: That seems the main advantage over the apprenticeship system at the big production houses, or the ABC, where one is narrowed to a specific job of writing without having the chance to explore the technical and formal aspects of the crafts...

Keith Thompson: Yes, and even less so now than when we were working for them. In those days, I think there really was something to be learnt from a *Homicide* episode.

The final fab four of the *Homicide* squad (1975)
L-R Dennis Grosvenor, Gary Day, Don Barker, Charles 'Bud' Tingwell

Keith Thompson: Structurally you could play with the rules and get something out of it. But "soap opera" is so much a committee process that there is less of a learning experience than on series dramas like the all-film *Homicides*. What we are getting now is a whole generation of writers growing up never having written "The End". In the old series, you created characters for your episode and it had an ending. Sure you couldn't experiment to a great extent, but at least at Crawfords you were able to slip something in every now and then, which is what Everett de Roche says.

Paul Davies: What happens when people come through the School and end up in the "Committee System".

Keith Thompson: One of last year's graduates is doing that already, at Grundy's. It's hard to say, but I think the process is valuable, for a year or so, if only for what seems to happen to the people who do it. The people who were there when we were are, now, six years later, commissioners of the AFC (Australian Film Commission) or producing a lot of film and television. It gives you a few names and that's of value, if nothing else. There is also the value of having your stuff played. You write a lot of material and see it on the screen very quickly. It's sort of like Kleenex Tissues – out once and thrown away. But you must learn something from that.

Paul Davies: Can we expect a challenge coming out of the School?

Keith Thompson: That is School policy. But, being realistic, the only way you can break the pattern of commercial television is to do so politically, through legislation.

Paul Davies: Is there no way of challenging the System in a qualitative sense?

Keith Thompson: You would hope so. You would hope the mini-series have started to do that. That is the ambition you have to believe in – if you didn't you would go crazy.

Paul Davies: What scripts are being developed at the School?

Keith Thompson: Of the three full-time students Cory Taylor has just finished *Fertility Rite,* a 50 minute television play which I think is one of the best I've read anywhere. The second year students used it as the basis of an actor/director workshop, two weeks' rehearsal and a week of putting it down on tape. I still think it's good enough to be done outside. In fact, it has already picked up some interest from actors who have workshopped it. I bring in actors and we just sit around and do script readings. It is important that each student gets the chance of having a 50 minute, personal statement-type play done.

Paul Davies: How does it work here in practice? Does a full time student director tell the writers "I want a film about so and so. Can you do it?", or does it go the other way, with a writer trying to sell his/her idea to the filmmaker?

Keith Thompson: I am trying to keep this as loose as possible. It certainly happens a lot, and directors say, "I want to do a film about this, but I can't write it." You then try to make a marriage with your writing students. I also feed it back the other way, and go to a student director and say "Have a look at this." The significance for the writer, again, is that you go right through the production process with it.

Paul Davies: Is the writer usually involved in a film's post-production?

Keith Thompson: As much as they can be. I want them also to direct their own material and see how that feels. Most of the writers in the full year will make a short video – whatever. We can't afford much, but they get to make something. This way, the whole process is demystified for them. When the technology is later thrown up as an obstacle, they know how to handle it. This applies more to television than film, because video development is racing ahead so much.

Paul Davies: Yet commercial television seems surprisingly slow to take advantage of it...

Keith Thompson: It gets back to visual consciousness. Scriptwriting is essentially about image against image, and not necessarily words (dialogue). How to get a visual vocabulary is something I am exploring here. My feeling, on one level, is that the writing students should spend half their time as say, film editors, because that's the beginning and the end of the process.

Paul Davies: Editing as a form of writing...

Keith Thompson: Yes. I have learnt a lot from going to double-heads (combined sound and picture editing sessions) and listening to soundtracks – not just the dialogue but the rest of the sound. As soon as you learn to use a sophisticated sound or visual track, you are saving on dialogue, on words. It is a basic structure that is the sort of area into which I am interested in pushing writers. It is difficult if you come out of a literary tradition, but then that's what scriptwriting is; it doesn't matter how the script actually reads. I have been making conscious efforts to get more emotion into the dialogue and change my style. That was one reason I came here. I started writing when I was at film school (Ravensbourne College, Kent) and stopped last year. That's 12 or 13 years of solid writing – the last six of seven professionally, and it all seemed part of the one process. It was one trip.

Paul Davies: So you wanted to make some sort of break?

Keith Thompson: That is what's happening now. I supposed I had idealized what the break might be, and I had fantasies about being charged up by heady students, from nine to five, then going home and doing a masterpiece or two in the evening. But that hasn't happened. I am exhausted by the "nine to five" and just want to go home to bed. But I did want the break, because I wanted to look at language, at style.

Paul Davies: Can you relate that to anything you are working on now?

Keith Thompson: It's hard to put into words, but I think the reason I stopped writing was because I had realized I had turned some corner. Maybe it scared me a bit. I realized the writing I could do from now on could actually come from inside me and I didn't need the prop of a particular series format or whatever that had sustained me through the years. I also believe there is a certain cumulative exhaustion that builds up over a certain time when you have had to write a lot of television. So I am just letting the projects that hang around my neck for years fade into the distance…I'll pick it up in a year or so, when I really want to start writing.

Paul Davies: How do you get an idea – and this relates to the students as well – where does it generate from?

Keith Thompson: For me the idea has always sprung out of character; it has always been based on an interchange between one character and another That has been the first sparking point for me. What I believe now is that there are more ideas around than there are people who can transpose them. I am particularly interested in structure, because structure is how you state the idea. This is something that is apparent from the amount of scripts that I have to read for recruitment here, and also because I have been on Creative Development panels for the AFC. I suppose I read about 400 scripts last year, a staggering amount. And you could say there would hardly a bad idea among them. The concepts are there in the first page synopsis, but it is the realization of the idea that is at fault. And realization is structure.

Paul Davies: Is that what the school is teaching?

Keith Thompson: Sure. I don't want to suggest that I am under-valuing ideas; I just want to explore the different ways of conceptualizing ideas into structure. I don't think an idea for me is ever dissociated from its emotional content. But this dissociation is evident in a lot of work in this country. It strikes me as a major problem. We are being "nine to five" about a lot of writing here. One has to find the metaphor, to find the lens that is going to take one's perception and invert it – as I did with *Gail.* I didn't want to write about a guy, so writing about a girl was like looking through the lens that inverts the image, that turns it upside down.

Paul Davies: And that gives you the distance, the objectivity to write?

Keith Thompson: It's not distance, I don't want distance, because it is important to be able to pour all the light through the lens. But it gives you the objectivity to look back into yourself somehow; the lens is the research period. Through the research period -which is vital - you find the structure of your lens, you find the quality of the lens that you are going to put your perception through so that it comes out differently.

Paul Davies: Is the lens your perspective of a technique?

Keith Thompson: It is technique, research. It is the filter through which you work. Somehow, maybe it changes from first person to third person.

Paul Davies: It is like when you start using "he" or "she" instead of "I". Until then, it is autobiography or diary writing...

Keith Thompson: Mike Jenkins was out last Friday, doing a seminar, and he made the terrific point about how, when you are actually at the typewriter "writing", it is not inside, but a sort of three-dimensional image dancing in front of you. It needs to be that much outside of you, but not distanced. It has to have that emotional quality because films are emotion.

Paul Davies: A feature these days seems to be about a three year project, especially if an individual is going to be involved right through. It is a huge commitment...

Keith Thompson: God knows why films take that long. I feel relatively confident with a 50 minute television single shot. I like that form and I know I can write it in a couple of months. But why do films take so long – and you are kidding yourself if you think it is anything less than a year. How writers sustain themselves through three year projects is really unexplored. I have been working the past couple of years on feature ideas and I am into them for a year at least, sometimes two, just on the script. I find it really debilitating when I am going further and further out on a limb, with no guarantee that when I have finished, it is going to get made. For a scriptwriter, just having the work here, watchable, reinforces a hell of a lot of conceptions about just what you think of yourself as a person, as a writer, and you buy into the feature number and you are away from that for two years. I haven't had anything made this decade.

Paul Davies: So how do you know when to stop, to give a particular project away?

Keith Thompson: It gets competitive with me: it is "it" or me, if it ever comes to a choice. I wish I knew the answer to that. There are projects where it would have been better for me to say "enough is enough". Another major problem with a lot of professional writers is that, if they have some sense of their own advancement, once

they have done something, they want to move onto something else And over
five or so years, you close certain doors; you narrow your possibilities; you have to
feel as a writer that you are getting better. That is the only thing that keeps you sane.
But getting better with narrower possibilities – that is a hassle.

**Paul Davies: Perhaps then, one function of the Open Program could be some
sort of consultancy service, where a number of people could look at a work...**

Keith Thompson: That's exactly what we should be doing. If something can be done
here on a portapak (small video camera) within the corridors of this building one
Saturday, then people could look at it and see it. It might give them the strength,
whatever, to go back and write it.

Paul Davies: It also gives you something to show somebody.

Keith Thompson: Yes it is a realization of your work.

**Paul Davies: Despite the technical competence of a lot of film school films, some
people seem uncertain about what they are trying to say. The tendency is to see
them as just technical exercises with no great ideas bursting through....**

Keith Thompson: There has to be a greater emphasis on the idea and on the
translation of that idea into film. The idea needs to be transposed in a strong way.
The actual idea's quality, I suppose is something that has been faulty. It is part of the
Writing Workshop's function to initiate that, and it hasn't been operating as such in
the past couple of years. I don't know the answer, but I think my function here is to
encourage people to work to the limits. It is not good enough for people to say, "Oh
look, I can do this type of film." The incentive should always be to work to the
limits, to find out what you didn't know you knew – that discovery of what all
writing's about.

Within the industry at large, there has always been that tendency to make films about
what you knew when you started; so, there is no discovery. Gutsiness of ideas, a
sophisticated world view is always linked to exploration and experimentation, and
maybe its absence is a manifestation of keeping things at arm's length and all those
other things I have mentioned.

I'd like to make a more cogent statement out of it, but I can't. All I can say is, this is
the place where we must begin to examine these issues. The Film School is the place
where the debate must start.

Thus far the effort to make the Writing Workshop more accessible seems to be
having distinct practical benefits. Other projects underway early this year include a
three week workshop with NIDA (National Institute for Dramatic Arts) students. The
effect of associating actors with writers/filmmakers has made the various groups
involved particularly aware of each other's respective needs and difficulties.

For the actors the ability to be involved in the development of a script was a novel one. Normally, they felt themselves merely the "interpreters" of something that is fixed. For writing student Ian David, the experience gave him the chance to determine just precisely how much information he can hand to an actor:

"When a writer gives a script to a person, and it goes wrong – in dialogue or some other sense – perhaps it is simply because he didn't give enough information, or because it was impossible for him to give that information. It is also important for the writer to know when to shut-up, because one can write something that sounds a bit flat, but in another person's hands suddenly it is vibrant and it works."

For their part the NIDA students felt film and television technicians rarely understood their particular difficulties as performers. The AFTS experience is seen as a first step towards overcoming this difficulty later on. They saw themselves as moving out into the industry in concert with the film students there are working with now. Despite management commitment to the formulas, they felt they could being the process of making the industrial, working situation a more "human" one.

Another film being shot at the moment, by third year director Di Priest, is based on a script by Nick Delaland, who has a background in theatre. Delaland sees the production of his script as a personal breakthrough. *Sam, Johnno, and... You* deals with the plight of a young man seeking work at an abattoir. It is a carefully observed and beautifully economic work with a great deal of emotional involvement that Keith Thompson says he is looking for.

Sam, Johnno, and... You has the potential to reverse the trend in film school films. Its characters come across as fully-realized people, and it doesn't hold issues at arm's length, because it has the validity of a certain "lived" experience. It therefore remains to be seen what next year's class of established novelists and playwrights, with the assistance of Keith Thompson, Austin Steele and the Literature Board, will actually come up with.

"How to get a visual vocabulary is something I am exploring here.
And it has to have that emotional quality because films are emotion."

Since this interview in 1981 Keith Thompson's later career has continued to flourish with scripts for the feature *Clubland*, starring Brenda Blethyn, which premiered at the 2007 Sundance Film Festival. It was sold to Warner Independent Pictures in one of the festival's biggest distribution deals.

Clubland (2007)
Emma Booth, Khan Chittenden, Brenda Belthyn

Clubland won the 2007 AWGIE (Australian Writer's Guild Award for Best Original Feature Film, the overall AWGIE for Outstanding Australian Script of the Year and was nominated for an AFI (Australian Film Institute) Award for Best Original Screenplay.

Keith also co-adapted Tony Brigg's stage play, *The Sapphires* which premiered at the 2012 Cannes Film Festival in a Special Midnight Screening.

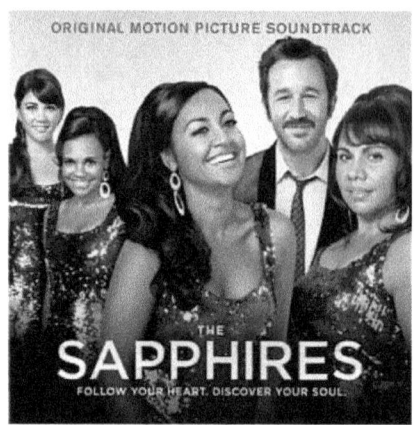

The Sapphires tells the story of a group of young Aboriginal singers recruited to perform in Vietnam in the late 1960s. It won two AWGIE Awards for Keith Thompson in 2012: Best Feature Film Adaptation and the overall AWGIE for Outstanding Australian Script of the Year. *The Sapphires* took home 11 AACTA awards in 2013, including Best Adapted Screenplay. Keith had previously won the overall AWGIE for Outstanding Australian Script of the Year in 1991 for an episode of the medical series GP.

ONCE UPON A TIME IN OZTRALIA
(Negotiating The Story On Australian Television)
Paul Davies
METRO # 124/125 (2000)

Nocturnal Emissions

In a couple of million years from now when an intelligent civilisation in a galaxy far, far away, finally manages to decipher the nocturnal emissions of Australian Television Drama (only just then reaching them on the cosmic internet) what will they make of life as it was lived at the end of the Twentieth Century on our island continent? Will they see these stories, this radio-borne, electronic time capsule as a representation of true events involving some long extinct carbon based life form? Or will they more correctly (being intelligent) read them as merely a simulacrum of what actually went on, a playful fabrication of the real? And will there be any way of charging them royalties for the privilege?- the ultimate futures' market!

Either way, these distant creatures will be confronted by a society that is clearly riven by crime, obsessed with bad health, and desperately seeking solace in any available capturing of "togetherness." Because Oztralian Television Drama as it has presented itself over its first half century (whether in series or serial form- and that distinction is increasingly blurred) slots basically and very neatly into three specific precincts of human behaviour : The Struggle For Justice (Cop Shows) The Search For A Cure (Medical Dramas) and Faith In The Community (Soap Operas).

Generally speaking (and ignoring for the moment the possibility of other genres such as Historical Dramas, School Stories and Kids' Shows), the above three are the broad parameters within which the quasi-mythical land of Oz resides. A place of rampant make-believe.

The modus operandi (to borrow a phrase) of the Cop and Medical shows depends fundamentally on "Action" to further their story arcs. A crime has to be solved, an illness must be treated. Whereas, the narrative engine of the Soaps rides more comfortably on the nuances of character and emotion as well as the eternal human road markers of birth, death, career, love and marriage. The more credibly the story is driven by its characters' innermost urges and desires the more convincing the Soap becomes. The alternative scenario is covered by the phrase "the plot creaks" – i.e. it announces itself as an extremely clumsy and mechanical narrative device. This is generally something to be avoided.

The Struggle For Justice

The Struggle For Justice is essentially where television drama in Oztralia all began. It was the crusading, one-set wonder: *Consider Your Verdict* that set the ball rolling with its weekly crime enacted retrospectively via the court case that followed. At the end of which the audience, as the title suggests, were invited to make up their own minds as to the guilt or innocence of the parties involved.

The courtroom set for *Consider Your Verdict*

This economical show, with its built-in audience involvement, proved successful enough to pave the way for the equally pioneering *Homicide* and its cousins: *Division Four, Matlock Police,* and *Cop Shop* (all Crawfords products of the late 60s, early 1970s). Since then, the Struggle for Justice has embraced all the chronicles of law and order, murder, robbery and mayhem as contained in *Hunter, Prisoner, Rafferty's Rules, The Magistrate, Water Rats, Murder Call, Stingers, State Coroner, Police Rescue, Phoenix, Janus, Wildside, Scales of Justice, Halifax FP, Good Guys/Bad Guys, Above The Law* and of course the three "Blues": *Bluey, Blue Murder,* and the phenomenally successful *Blue Heelers.*

By 1973, at the end of George Mallaby's six years at Homicide, Crawfords had three hits on its hands: *Homicide*, *Matlock Police* and *Division 4*. *Crawford Productions Pty Ltd/National Film and Sound Archive*

George Mallaby in *Homicide*

This string of titles exhibits little potential for running out of steam with many clever variations on the common theme. For example *Stingers* dips into the murky world of undercover cops. *Water Rats* treats the audience to police work on the delightful, overseas-sales-inducing backdrop of Sydney harbour. *Murder Call* harks back to the old *Homicide* formula with its discovery of the body in the first three minutes (the "teaser") and its determination to solve the crime much like an Agatha Christie/Sherlock Holmes saga.

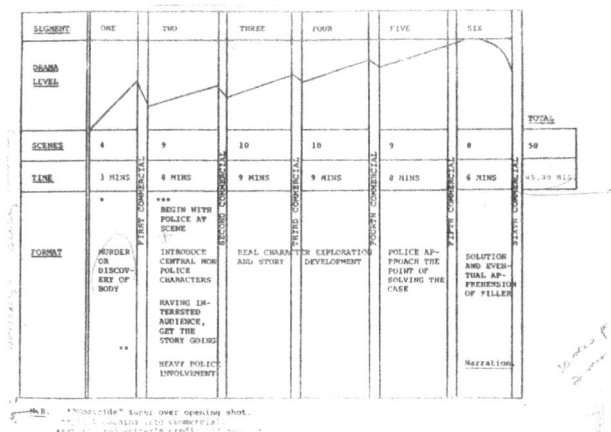

The highly successful *Homicide* script template
Drama levels rise towards each ad break

The Search For A Cure

The obsession with the deteriorating carbon based, human life-form itself, the Search For A Cure genre, is represented by the agonies, ecstasies, frantic decision making and sometimes bad end results of all the medical shows that now include (again by no means exhaustively): *Medivac, All Saints, Country Practice, State Coroner, Halifax FP* and of course the 3 Doctors: *GP* (city doctors), *Young Doctors,* and *Flying Doctors.*

Several *Young Doctors* (1976 -1983)

It will be seen immediately that there are already crossovers happening here. *State Corner* and *Halifax FP* by definition straddle both the crime and health genres. Just as *Medivac*, while notionally a hospital drama necessarily also involves a constant engagement with all sorts of emergency services including police, ambulance drivers and helicopter pilots (see also in this respect the two "Skies" series: *Skyways* and *Big Sky* - a sub genre perhaps?) to which *Police Rescue* also partially belongs. Because, while *Police Rescue* announces itself as primarily a cop show, it nevertheless deals with people being rescued from cliff faces, who optimally have some connection to a crime, are in need of transport by helicopter, and are therefore ultimately thrown back again on the tender mercies of that deteriorating hospital system. A brilliant trifecta of concerns that qualifies *Police Rescue* for inclusion in two major genres and one sub-genre (Cops, Doctors and Pilots).

Faith In The Community

Standing in direct opposition to the dysfunctional lifestyles of the medical and legal fraternities is the soothing relief and reassurances of the Faith In The Community option. Here we find the remaining gang of major players including the fondly remembered and seminal *Bluebird,* the raunchy, envelope-pushing *Number 96,* the global and ubiquitous juggernaut of *Neighbours,* plus of course *The Box, Home and Away, Sons and Daughters, In Between, Dogs Head Bay, Sea Change, Something In The Air, Going Home,* and the Gold Coast duo: *Paradise Beach* and *Pacific Drive.*

Main Cast *Something In The Air* (2000 - 2002)

The "Community" as such can be organised along architecturally vertical lines (*No. 96* was an actual apartment block, *In Between* set in a housing commission highrise, *The Box* - a television station) or distributed geographically along a particular suburban street as in *Pacific Drive* (literally) and *Neighbours'* famous Ramsay Street. More typically the "Community" encompasses an entire town or village (e.g. *Seachange's* Pearl Bay or *Something In The Air's* Emu Springs). With *Going Home* the Community is a bunch of office workers doing their daily commute on a suburban train. In *Above The Law* the producers have brilliantly sited the Community <u>above</u> an actual police station, thus managing to straddle (literally and very conveniently) two major precincts of behaviour without even having to go outside the front door!

In all cases the Community as such attempts to meld the inclusiveness of the city (where strangers are usually welcome) with the familiarity of the village (where strangers are generally pretty well deeply frowned upon).

In the Community shows people are gentler and more stereotypically Oztralian (along lines long since laid down by Henry Lawson, Steele Rudd and Banjo Paterson- the "bush battler" archetype). In these examples the story is mostly framed by the common theme of yearning for something better; of seeking a more meaningful existence inside an ideal society of neighbours, relatives and friends who fundamentally like each other and whose financial, sexual and emotional lives are intricately and supportively entwined. (In *Pacific Drive* they tended to loathe each other but this was an exceptional show in many other ways too.)

In holding out the hope of a better life, the Community shows appeal directly to the urban alienation and dislocation of their core city audiences. The City turns to The Country as a source of "communality"- that prehistoric human craving for a bond established beyond family lines towards a kind of "tribal" experience- something that living an atomised life in the suburban wastelands has generally robbed people of (apart from the once suburban, now nationalised, soon to be globalised, local footy team). All of which is as close to a spiritual formulation as Oztralian TV Drama seems to get (always remembering that the village or street also has its resident priest e.g. Father Brian in *Something In The Air*).

Community shows (Soaps) enshrine a feel good ambience in contrast to the constant terrors and chaos held in store by the Justice and Medical genres. Interestingly, there has also been a recent drift away from the inland setting (*Bellbird, A Country Practice*) towards locating it more directly on the coast (*Paradise Beach, Sea Change, Pacific Drive, Dogs Head Bay, Headland*).

Pacific Drive 1996-1997

This new retreat to the seaside perhaps mirrors the general decline of rural Oztralia and probably foreshadows the intention of the baby boomers who create and finance these shows to spend their looming retirements within earshot of some stretch of idyllic beach - preferably in Byron Bay or Port Douglas - places to which the location budget currently won't stretch.

Generic Pastiche

Of course there are many overlaps between the Community ethos and both the Cop and Doctor genres. *A Country Practice* obviously combines medical issues with a bucolic theme. Just as *Matlock Police* anticipated *Blue Heelers* by more than a decade in situating its essential police focus inside the supportive and reassuring confines of a small country town.

Indeed, the main tendency at the end of the century seems to involve an untidy scramble to include as many generic paradigms in any new series as is practically (and credibly possible) - with most shows now managing to straddle at least two or more camps. *Something In The Air* while overwhelmingly a Faith in the Community show nevertheless has a resident doctor and at least one *ex-* cop in the form of the publican, Stuart "Roo" McGregor. It also bucks the drift to the coast by being located unashamedly, almost daringly, in a financially declining ex-gold mining town.

Similarly *Sea Change*, while quintessentially expressing bucketloads of Faith In The Community, nevertheless pins its major plot formulations on the activities of a local magistrate, who is herself a refugee from the chaos and stress of the city. Each episode necessarily involves some scenes in her courtroom although this set is by no means as central to that show as it was in *Consider Your Verdict* (where it was the only set) or *Rafferty's Rules* where it was the main set .

Rafferty's Rules was also notionally a Crime show but was self-consciously located in the Sydney beachside suburb of Manly - almost prefiguring the drift to the coast a decade before the general rush began (and as a bonus could also offer tantalizing glimpses of that bankable harbour). However *Rafferty's Rules* never did fully exploit the quirky character potential of its Manly inhabitants as much as say, *Blue Heelers* does with the residents of Mt. Thomas or *Something In the Air* with the delightfully varied denizens of Emu Springs.

Likewise, another seminal series *The Sullivans,* while essentially historical in its focus (The Harking Back To a Halcyon Past genre), might also be included in the Community category because the primary site of its drama was the leafy Melbourne suburb of Camberwell and all the war affected people living there.

The Sullivans (1976 – 1983)
The Sullivan family outside their Camberwell weatherboard

Character Point Of View

In The Struggle For Justice the progression of the plot must be viewed essentially from the police point of view. This has two important consequences: 1) it never allows the audience to get ahead of the handful of core police characters (the "star vehicles") and 2) it makes for an intense focus on the serial-like intrigues, loves, ill health and personal challenges of these people. In *Blue Heelers* what happens to Tom or PJ, Dash or Maggie, is almost as important as the crime that week itself. Sometimes even more so (such as when PJ and Maggie become trapped together in a gold mine and finally consummate their URST - UnResolved Sexual Tension).

Concentration on the central characters also simplifies the storylining process and is generally assumed to engender viewer loyalty. The "what-will-happen-next-week" factor becomes heightened when it is regularly limited to the familiar four or five main players. The crimes and their perpetrators become subservient to the ongoing interest in the "story arcs" of the cops themselves. Consequently scriptwriters rarely get to extend their talents to embrace any personally invented and temporary new characters.

For all these reasons the story shapes and forms that are nocturnally emitted consist essentially of the same basic handful of dramatic chords played endlessly on the great piano of each show's Story Department. And here we come to the nub of the matter.

Owning The Story

If the genre is a given and there are only a very limited number of those (despite the crossovers), how does the story of each individual episode get manufactured within the formula? And who owns the plot that emerges ? Who essentially creates it (and therefore stands to benefit financially)? Especially considering that the writer is invisible to the process and anecdotal evidence suggests a fair swag of the audience believe the actors make up the lines themselves ! (For a classic example of the pitfalls of letting actors make up the dialogue themselves watch any episode of the maddeningly repetitive *Wildside.*)

What Wildside? Yes *Wildside.* Really? *Wildside*? Yes! *Wildside* !
(1997-1999)
Tony Martin and Rachael Blake

The difficulty of teasing out the various creative threads contributing to the narrative architecture of any episode of Oztralian Television was revealed in June this year via a dispute between The Australian Writer's Guild and Screen Producers Association before the Arbitration Commission. The issue concerned intellectual ownership of the Storyline and who contributed what exactly to its emergence on episodes of *Something In The Air.* The Hon. R. J. Garlick. found that "On any reasonable reading of the material before me the Writers have made a substantive contribution at the Story Conference even though it is a contribution which on the evidence before me cannot be apportioned in exact percentages between them and others." ("Others" being the Production Company as represented by the Story Editor, Script Editor and Researchers.)

He went on to say that the "...opposed positions of the parties exemplify the difficulties of assessing the value of contributions to the creative process in sophisticated but meaningful terms for the purposes of the arcane world of the law of contract."

The Scriptwriting Process

This testifies to the intensely collaborative nature of Television Scriptwriting. The plot of any given Series, whatever category it belongs to - whether The Struggle for Justice, Search For A Cure, or Faith In The Community - is almost always the outcome of a committee process that starts with "The Script Conference."

This takes place over one or two days (if its going badly) and its participants include a Story Editor (responsible for forward planning and 'big picture' issues), A Script Editor (a combined critic/script doctor with a good handle on the macro story thus far), a Writer (the ravaged looking functional alcoholic glooming uneasily in the corner), a Researcher (police specialist for cop shows, medical expert for hospital dramas), a Note-taker, sometimes the Producer/Line Producer, and occasionally a Network Executive (if things are going really, really badly).

Everybody except the Writer is on a salary, works out of the central office, is close to the action and keeps their ears firmly to the ground (which is not easy when you're also trying to run a word processor). The Writer is almost always a free lancer, worried about where the next contract is coming from, and belongs to one of three mysterious white board categories known (only to an inner sanctum) as the "A list" the "B list" and the "Black List." (Although members of the latter faction tend, by definition, not to make it to Story Conferences in the first place - unless things are going really really badly and the Story Department is truly desperate).

At the end of those one or two intensive plotting days a document called a "Story Line" is produced. As defined by the Series and Serials Agreement between the Writer's Guild and the Screen Producers, 'The Story Line' is a "written synopsis of the story in narrative form providing sufficient detail so that the essential dramatic development and main characters can be identified..."

With this document in hand the writer leaves his first invoice behind and, like an architect with a client's brief, goes home to turn what is essentially a page or so into about ten pages of narrative prose called the 'Scene Breakdown'. This is defined by the same Agreement as "the scenes in narrative form of the entire story indicating the fuller structure and development and characterisation of the plot."

And when (with many adjustments via emails, faxes, and phone calls back and forth) the 'Scene Breakdown' is finally given the green light the writer may get started on the first of usually two full Drafts. When the ratings are going fairly well the Networks tend to leave their Story Departments well alone and everyone luxuriates in a certain freedom to explore the full potential of the characters - within of course, the known and accepted parameters of the show's "Formula"- as outlined in its "Bible." "The Bible" documents a show's core cast along with their backgrounds, the setting, locations available and strict time limits in which any episode may happen (42 minutes of drama per TV hour for commercial networks, 48-50 minutes for the ABC/SBS)

In this way a "Release Script" finally emerges from the scrum ready for shooting and it is produced along lines firmly established through decades of industrial practice. While the writer has many expressive possibilities within the structural envelope of a given story line or a body of dialogue (bearing in mind all the other constraints of cast size, time slot censorship, number of sets, locations available, in-house style and formulas etc.) almost no television episode is the outcome of any single individual. Although a maimed handful of "bankable" writers may be so privileged - sometimes with indifferent results.

The Road Ahead

The question might therefore reasonably be asked: why so many cops, lawyers and doctors? What is it about these two professions that make them so disproportionately dominant on our small screens ? And will it ever be any different ? Why not builder's labourers, bank tellers, cooks, hairdressers or hotel managers- with all their attendant mingling in the common flow ?

Clearly the answer lies somewhere in the idea that crime and illness are by their nature life altering events and hence they carry the greater dramatic quotient. The experiences of police and medical officers necessarily imply a lot of climactic/dramatic action which can be accounted for in simple sets (the interview room, the hospital ward). Drama comes with the territory. It is simply easier to concoct scenarios out of the twin emergencies of breaking the law and getting sick (preferably both).

But it's not just the plot, it's how you tell it. And herein lies the creative possibility for any writer. Bearing in mind that series and serials now run to hundreds, if not thousands of episodes, contemporary scriptwriters are engaged in a kind of collective, macro-story telling that has no real literary precursor- with the possible exception perhaps of the serialised novels of authors such as Charles Dickens and more recently Armistead Maupin. Even so, the sheer quantity of material being produced for television far outweighs in story content and consumption time what any novel or even series of novels can offer. Sometimes Oztralian serials display a character's life story over a period of years that almost chronologically recreates a real time scenario. (c/f Julia Rutherford's mature age pregnancy in *Something In The Air* virtually takes almost nine months of programming to full term.)

In the Community genre the plot is carried more readily on the vagaries of character and a shared idea of what makes us human - the helping and supportive ethos as opposed to the more destructive and damaging predicaments of the criminal and the seriously ill. In this sense the Soaps actually offer, on the face of it, a greater hope for change, a wider scope for exploring all the principals of story form and character eccentricity.

If an Episode's "Story" is essentially the *What* happens and its "Structure" relates to *When* things happen; then a show's "Formula" is the *How* it happens, the "Characters" *Who* it happens to, and the "Dialogue" reveals *Why* it happens. Thus, in manufacturing drama on television we are dealing with a creative enterprise which advances along many separate but interconnected prongs. Everyone starts with a road map (the Storyline) but is invited to explore the detours (the Drafting). How a Story actually turns out can be deflected by a slight shift in character, a slip of the tongue, or a chance accident. Like life itself, writing is a journey and the fun of it sometimes lies in not knowing exactly how it will all end up. Although in Oztralian television the ending is generally fixed from the storyline stage. Always, from the writer's point of view, it's not the plot you're given but how you tell it.

Another unwritten law of television drama relates to the fact that no matter what journey a core character takes in any given episode they must end up (personality-wise at least) essentially back where they started (certainly by the end of that week on air.) In how many shows is the pub the definitive location ? In how many episodes does the teary scene come just before the end]? In Oztralia no macro change seems possible. URST (unresolved sexual tension) between male and female leads must remain just that: unresolved - otherwise the core reason around which that relationship endlessly turns begins to implode and it's dramatic raison d'etre evaporates (c/f Diver Dan and Laura Gibson finally getting horizontal in *Sea Change* only just before David Wenham decides to leave the series.)

Of course it can be argued that this is what real life is like anyway. Once our personalities are set down in childhood they are fixed for the long haul. The child being father/mother to the man/woman. Art imitating Life imitating Art.

"Reality" (sic) TV ?

Which raises the disturbing spectre of "Reality TV": the "observational docu/drama," the fly-on-the-wall camera, the *Sylvania Waters* model. Here is an example of a future "television entertainment" in which the scriptwriter we've come to know and love is finally absent from the process. In which the dramatic displacement of reality which we've been getting so far comes back to its first principals, almost by default. In which our confused soul mates in other galaxies far far away will finally be unable to untangle the found event from the constructed one.

Could this be the end towards which "The Story" on Oztralian Television is eventually heading? Towards a kind of de-manufactured ("amanufactured" ?) reality state? In which the audience become merely voyeurs on other people's (edited) lives. Television as an endless *Truman* (True - Man) *Show*. My hunch (and hope) is that people will still want the craft of fiction to shape meaning from the endless flow. And until computers develop souls writers are still the best workers qualified for the task of "lying the truth."

In short, the more things change the more they stay the same. And unless audiences demand otherwise it's difficult to imagine any better outcome. Once a successful show's formula is locked in (*Homicide, The Sullivans, Blue Heelers, Sea Change*) it generally doesn't budge. Networks focus with clinical precision on the ratings, but do the raw numbers tell us anything about the "quality" of the viewing? Is it sometimes more rewarding to have an actively engaged, albeit smaller, audience than a half brain-dead larger one? And despite some desperate attempts to find one, no Network executive yet has a crystal ball. And in this possibility lies the ongoing hope that something new *can* still happen. The generic templates may be set but success always lies in how you tweak them. Everyone is looking for that golden riff of characters and setting that fires the popular imagination.

Will the future viewers see it that way - the ones out there in the cosmos, as yet unborn? Or will they be asking their own version of Phillip Adams' famous question: "Is this really 50 years of Oztralian television - or just the same year over and over again?"

HEARING VOICES
Elizabeth Huntley
METRO #134 (2001)

"The reward I get is being able to think myself into the characters and
actually hear their voices in my head."

Elizabeth Huntley trained as a teacher at La Trobe University, and performed
Disability Support Work at the North Melbourne Institute of TAFE before
attending screenwriting courses at both Open Channel and the Australian Film
and Television School. She worked as a production assistant on Sharon
Connolly's *Nice Girls Like Us* and then as a research assistant for the La Trobe
University Media Production Unit. She has since written for several children's
television series including *Driven Wild, Driven Crazy* and *Chuck Finn.*
Subsequently, Elizabeth became a regular writer on the ABC series *Something
In The Air* and has also worked on the apparently endless Australian serial,
Neighbours,.

Paul Davies: How did you get into writing for television ?

Elizabeth Huntley: I joined a writing group doing a Dip Ed at La Trobe. I
wrote a one act play which people liked and responded to. I particularly liked
the idea of writing for voices. A year later, Rosa Colossimo, who was one of the

group and who later made the film *Moving Out,* asked me to submit some ideas to a producer she was then working for. This was a 10BA project - a telemovie - but that scheme eventually folded and the film unfortunately didn't get made. I did a few more things for her but nothing came of it. Then I thought of doing more of my own stuff and James Clayden, a director, asked me if I'd be interested in scripting a children's movie he'd been working on. I had a look at what he'd done, but it didn't relate to anything I felt I could do. So he asked if there was something in my experience I'd like to work on. And this made me think about my own childhood and I came up with an idea for a film which I still haven't managed to get made, but which I put about 10 years of my life into.

Paul Davies: What was that called ?

Elizabeth Huntley: *The Bush Billy.* It was based on my childhood growing up on a farm on the Mornington Peninsula in Victoria. The script has changed so much over the ten years I've been working on it. But it was a fantasy story set around my family. I got some initial funding from the AFC to write a treatment and then I took it to Bob Weiss. He optioned it for a number of years and we worked on various drafts together.

Paul Davies: It went into development hell ?

Elizabeth Huntley: Yes. It fell into that problem where the special effects became too expensive.

Paul Davies: This is the fantasy element ?

Elizabeth Huntley: Yes. It grew and grew. It didn't start out all that much as a fantasy. Bob pushed the fantasy element and wanted to develop that. He wanted it to be more of an action adventure. So it kept growing and growing and I think it outgrew the original size of the idea. And I didn't know enough about what I was doing at that stage. However, thanks to that project I learnt a huge amount about writing. Unfortunately, it went on for so long that I started to lose confidence. So the move into television has helped enormously in terms of bypassing what I felt was my falling into a bit of a black hole with writing. It even got to a point where I was wondering whether I should even pursue this career (laughs).

Paul Davies: How did the television work come about ?

Elizabeth Huntley: Somebody I knew was working at *Neighbours* as a script editor. They actually had a job going as a storyliner. I didn't know a lot about how TV worked, but I bowled up and then realised I hadn't done enough research on the programme. I hadn't seen enough of it on air. You really need to know a programme to function effectively in that kind of job. I felt I'd much rather be on the writing end of it anyway, so they gave me an audition script and they liked what I did. Then they offered me a couple of episodes but I think I got bogged down in the timing. I didn't realise how critical that was. How each segment (the bits between the ads) had to be exactly 7 or 8 minutes long.

Neighbours – Kylie Minogue and Jason Donovan tie the knot

Paul Davies: So on *Neighbours* a writer is handed a complete scene breakdown ?

 Elizabeth Huntley: Yes. You just do the one draft and you're given 10 days - which I thought was only a short amount of time. But I now realise that was a total luxury (laughs). I quite enjoyed it except that I kept getting bogged down in this timing thing.

Paul Davies: What was the problem there ? Your timings were out ?

Elizabeth Huntley: Yes. And in order to get the timings right I became obsessed with going back and editing and then editing and editing to try and get it down. But I think I thereby destroyed what I had written. So it really came across as being very constipated. And they ended up saying to me: "we just don't know what's happened to you because we really liked what you did at first". I was also pretty appalled when I saw what I'd done on air.

Paul Davies: Can you talk about that ?

Elizabeth Huntley: I think it was just the shock of seeing actors speaking your words. It made me realise how some of the things you imagined were going to work and be spoken in a certain way end up being spoken in an entirely different way.

Paul Davies: Were they the same words at least ?

Elizabeth Huntley: Some of them. Some had been edited and changed. I thought some of it had really worked fantastically. But other bits you think - if I'd been the director I would have done that scene very differently.

Paul Davies: Is this a problem built into the nature of television writing ? That the writer sits alone at home all the time ? Away from the set...

Elizabeth Huntley: Well I think with a show like *Neighbours* it would be very difficult to involve the writer anyway. They have to keep such a tight rein on everything. But certainly, ideally, I think it would be fantastic if the writer was able to follow through with the script. As far as I know in the past, writers used to be there to take a script right through to production. I remember Gwenda Marsh telling me about that kind of thing at Crawfords.

Paul Davies: And then after *Neighbours* ?

Elizabeth Huntley: Bob Weiss teamed me up with David Rapsey to progress *The Bush Billy* idea but by then I was losing heart with the project. As it turned out, however, David was producing a children's TV series called *Driven Crazy* for Barron Films. They had a script that had fallen into difficulty and they only had the money for a writer to do one draft. So David asked me to do that, which I did. Which I really enjoyed. That series was finally produced and screened in 1999. That lead to another script on the second series called *Driven Wild* which was script produced by Ysabelle Dean. She proved to be a terrific support for me because she sat me down and went through the scripts I was writing and pointed out fairly obvious things that I hadn't caught up with. And so via Ysabelle, I then got jobs on two of the *Chuck Finn* series which was also a Barron production.

Paul Davies: What was the concept behind the *Driven Crazy/Driven Wild* series ?

Elizabeth Huntley: It was about a father who was a bit of a nomad with his two kids. They were travelling Victoria, going from town to town in a huge old car. He was a jack of all trades and the kids didn't go to any regular school. The girl was 15 and the boy, who was younger did a correspondence course. Their education - or lack of it - was always a bit of an issue and they would tap into schools along the way, depending on where the father got work. So it was about fitting in. I enjoyed writing it. Though I would have enjoyed it more if I'd felt more confidant of myself as a writer. But that's where Ysabelle was such a great help.

Paul Davies: And *Chuck Finn* ? This sounds like a bad run of luck going back to the *Bush Billy* saga.

Elizabeth Huntley: Yes. In fact, in 1998 I worked on another series for Barron Entertainment developed by Carol Drouyn called *Wild Kat* and that came to grief too. I wrote one episode but as soon as I finished writing it, the production came to a halt.

Paul Davies: Then you started writing *Something In The Air* ?

Elizabeth Huntley: Yes. Just before the *Chuck Finn* series came along I worked on *Something In The Air*. Which was a terrific experience. I worked with Adam Todd, Jenny Sharp and Kirsty Fisher as editors. I wrote five blocks all up. That's like 10 half hour episodes. It was the first adult show I'd worked on.

Paul Davies: What are the differences writing for kids as opposed to adult drama ?

Main Cast for *Something In the Air* (2000 -2002)

Elizabeth Huntley: I think the kids' drama is harder. When I started on *Something In the Air* I expected it to be much more difficult writing for adults. But in fact, I was amazed to find it was easier. With dialogue for example you've got a lot more leeway. In children's drama a lot of it has to be very action specific and entertaining in a way that doesn't come all that easily.

Paul Davies: Do you cast yourself back to when you had your own children ?

Elizabeth Huntley: Yes. Well I do. (laughs) But there's a bit of a danger in that because my sons are grown up now and it would be getting a bit old fashioned to cast back to when they were young. But I find myself catching up with neighbours' kids. And of course I'm constantly eavesdropping on conversations. Hearing the latest expressions and so on.

Paul Davies: Do you find yourself keeping a little notebook ?

Elizabeth Huntley: I do. And frequently I've got pieces of paper in my handbag with snippets written all over them. And then I forget about them of course and ages later they pop up again...(laughs) I've also got a file of weird and wonderful pieces of paper - random ideas.

Paul Davies: And so *Something In the Air* also came to an end unfortunately.

Elizabeth Huntley: Yes. Indeed. At the moment I'm waiting to do something on a film idea that I've been working on with James Clayden. Which is like going in circles back to where it all started. It's called *The Unidentified Woman* . An idea that James has been working on for a few years. And he asked me if I'd be interested in trying to do something with it. There's no funding yet. But we're waiting to hear.

Paul Davies: *Something In The Air* was a Simpson Le Measurier/ ABC coproduction. Is there a difference working on a show like that compared to writing for commercial networks ?

Elizabeth Huntley: It's hard to compare because with children's television, which is where I worked with the commercial networks, there are a lot of rules and regulations anyway. In terms of language, the material you deal with. And also because a lot of those programmes were quite ambitious in what they would like, ideally, to use in terms of special effects. So you're very conscious of budgets. You have to realise extraordinary ideas with quite modest resources.

Paul Davies: The ABC would also be pretty cash strapped wouldn't it ?

Elizabeth Huntley: Yes. I found when I was doing *Something In the Air* that a lot of things you wanted to put in just couldn't happen because we couldn't afford it.

Paul Davies: Is that a problem or a challenge for a writer ?

Elizabeth Huntley: Sometimes it's frustrating, but sometimes you also find it can work better if you think about it in a different way. It really depends. There are times when you think something is going to work in a particular way and when you see it made you realise it would have been better if you'd gone for something simpler. What you sometimes see on the screen often defeats the purpose of having attempted it in the first place.

Paul Davies: As I understand it, a lot of *Something In The Air* was often done with one take. So it was more a matter of just - get the lines right and that's it. It's remarkable it achieved the quality it did.

Elizabeth Huntley: Yes. It is. It was a really nice show to work on. It was hard at first though. The first episode I wrote there I thought it was really pretty awful - watching it back on air. And I didn't anticipate they'd ever give me any more work. It was the episode about the Olympic torch coming through Emu Springs. And the problem was they had to rethink the story a lot because they kept getting feedback from the legal department that you couldn't do this... and you couldn't do that... There was an issue of copyright around the torch itself.

Paul Davies: I remember that episode. The torch ended up looking like a milk shake container with a jam tin on top.

Elizabeth Huntley: (laughs) Yes. And I think that, as a result, the story ended up being all over the place. Not really hanging together. The plot definitely fell apart.

Paul Davies: Which is hardly your fault...

Elizabeth Huntley: No. Except it was my fault that I wasn't as experienced as I should have been.

Paul Davies: But they liked it enough to offer you four more blocks.

Elizabeth Huntley: Yes. And that was fantastic. The show was a very rewarding experience and I just wished it had been able to keep on going.

Paul Davies: What is it that attracts you to writing for the box - given it's such a rocky road - with the uncertainty of shows coming to grief financially, the difficulty raising money and so on...

Elizabeth Huntley: I think it's because writing for television is the only thing I've ever found that I'm any good at. (laughs) That I also enjoy doing. The reward I get is being able to think myself into the characters and actually hear their voices in my head. And with a little bit of help I translate that onto the page. If I clearly hear the voices, though - it doesn't always happen - but with *Something In The Air* you get to know the characters so well that it becomes quite effortless. At other times you're struggling to find the character. But once you do it's really a rewarding process.

Paul Davies: Is it a matter of research. Just watching the show ?

Elizabeth Huntley: Well *Something In the Air* hadn't been to air when I wrote my first episode. So I don't know quite how well I had the characters down that first time at all. But then, yes, I watched it and became very familiar with the actors. And also reading other people's scripts helped.

Paul Davies: Do you have a day structure to how you work ?

Elizabeth Huntley: For me it's pretty random because I tend to be undisciplined unless I'm working to a deadline. I get very disciplined if I have a deadline. In which case I switch on the computer about 8.30 am and work right through. I should probably restrict myself a bit. I tend to work through till four in the afternoon. But as time runs out I will work day and night. It also depends on how familiar I am with the series. In the end, with *Something In The Air*, I found I could do it a lot faster. So you tend to relax a bit about the time available. With the first one I wasn't sure I was even going to be able to do it. The time allowance seemed very tight (a week for the scene breakdown, two weeks to take two half-hour episodes to first draft).

Paul Davies: Do you feel the writer in television is given due recognition ?

Elizabeth Huntley: Writers don't get a lot of recognition. I notice it more in regard to film than television. I know they don't in TV. But in television it's such a kind of group thing anyway. You're part of a team and there are so many people. So much can change from the time it leaves your hands to what comes up on screen. It changes - not because someone doesn't like what you've done, but out of necessity. It all has to conform to the story line before or after your particular episode. But even in film, writers have a hard time. Some do get recognition of course. But on the whole they don't. Films tend to be associated more with directors. A film by... and so on. It astounds me sometimes that you practically have to search to find out who wrote something - for their credit. But the whole thing may have been that writer's original idea. They may have put years of work into it, plus a lot of their personal life. Then they've given the director the blue print. And the writer hardly rates a mention. It seems unfair but that's what happens to writers all the time.

(Interview held at *Tamani Café*, Lygon Street Carlton, 22 October 2001)

A DIFFERENT WAY OF LOOKING
Mark Shirrefs
METRO #133 (2001)

> "So long as you don't encourage our children to kill their parents, everything will be fine ..."
>
> Editorial feedback from the Head of the Shanghai Film Studio to Mark Shirrefs and John Thomson on their scripts for *Land Of The Dragon Lord*

Mark Shirrefs and John Thomson are two of Australia's most successful creators of children's television. The seven series they've collaborated on so far include: *The Girl From Tomorrow*, *Tomorrow's End*, *Mission: Top Secret*, *Spellbinder*, *Land Of The Dragon Lord*, *Let The Blood Run Free*, and most recently, *Pig's Breakfast*. Both *The Girl From Tomorrow* and *Spellbinder* have also been adapted to novels. In co-production deals with European networks and the Shanghai Film Studio, some of these series have reached audiences measured, potentially, in the hundreds of millions. *Spellbinder* also garnered an AWGIE for its creators, as well as two ATOM Awards and an AFI Award.

Mark Shirrefs trained as an actor at the Victorian College of the Arts, then co-founded the Flying Fruit Fly Circus and directed plays for the Murray River Performing Group and TheatreWorks (including the long running location theatre piece, *Storming Mont Albert By Tram*). He graduated from the Swinburne School of Film and Television in 1985. In partnership with director Kathy Mueller and executive producer Ron Saunders, Mark and John Thomson created *The Girl From Tomorrow* series for the 9 Network. Currently, Mark, John and Noel Price are developing a new children's series for possible co-production in China. Mark also lectures in creative writing at RMIT (Melbourne).

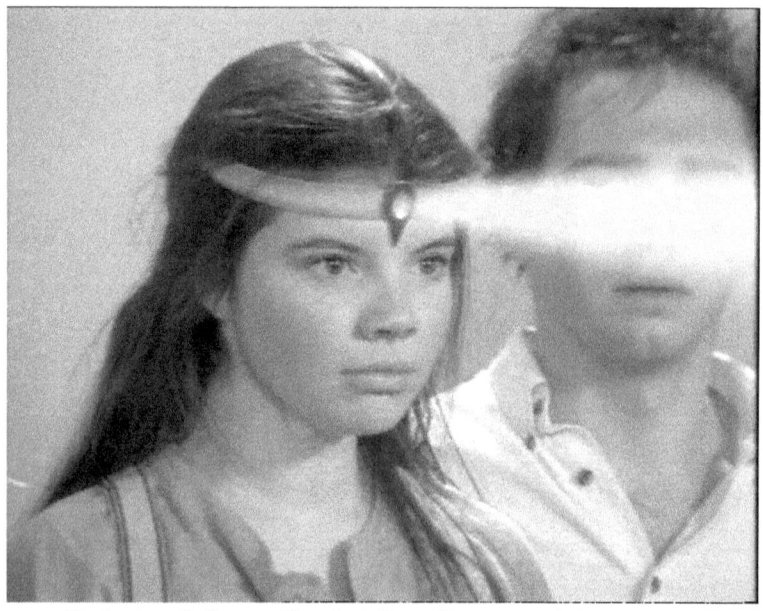

Katharine Cullen as *The Girl From Tomorrow* (1991 – 1993)

Paul Davies: How did the acting and theatre work translate into a job writing for television?

Mark Shirrefs: John Thomson, Ian Mortimer and Boris Connolly created a clown show which John, Ian and myself turned into a screenplay called *The Magic Telescope*. This project actually got quite a substantial amount of development funding from the Children's Television Foundation and the NSW FTO. The money came not only to write a script, but also to do a full budget and build scale models for the set. It was a children's fantasy adventure story. It was very expensive and nobody wanted to take it on (we're still hoping), but with the script at least, we finally had an example of our work to show to people. While trying to attract a producer for the project, we met up with Kathy Mueller, who had been a student with John and I at the VCA and was by then living in Sydney. She had been offered a gig by Film Australia to direct a series called *The Girl From Tomorrow*. This hadn't been written yet, but she convinced Ron Saunders that John and I could do it. So he commissioned us to write a pilot episode, which he used to raise the budget. John, Kathy and I developed a bible for the show and by the time we'd got the money, we'd been funded for three scripts, which were all eventually produced. *The Girl From Tomorrow* was successful enough to lead to a second series called *Tomorrow's End*, which was produced and directed by the line producer from the first series, Noel Price. Noel then began working for Grundy's on a children's series called *Mission: Top Secret*, which involved about half a dozen European countries. John and I wrote four half hour episodes for that (subtitled *The Polish Pony Puzzle*). So we got the proverbial phone call from overseas, but it wasn't from Hollywood, it was from Poland.

Paul Davies: A lot of the work you and John have produced has been in co-production with either European or Asian companies. How does the co-production deal affect the writing of a project?

Mark Shirrefs: The most difficult aspect is that you have a whole lot more people looking at your work. The hardest example was *Land Of The Dragon Lord*, which required both Chinese and Polish elements.

Land of the Dragon Lord (1997)

Paul Davies: How do you mix Polish and Chinese threads in a single narrative?

Mark Shirrefs: The best way is to go to these countries first. *Spellbinder* wouldn't have worked unless we'd actually gone to Poland. You see stuff. We saw a guy in China riding a bicycle with a fridge tied to the side and that gave us an idea for a scene. We had network involvement in both China and Poland. We thought we might have trouble in China, but they were very easygoing. We were at a dinner with the Shanghai Film Studio people once and we'd had no feedback about the scripts at all so we asked them what they thought. And after a moments consultation with his partner, the head of the Shanghai Film Studio turned back to John and me and said: 'We have heard that you are very good television writers. As long as you do not encourage our children to kill their parents, we're sure it will be fine'. [laughs] That was the extent of the feedback from China. The Polish connection was very different. We worked with a Polish dramaturge. He looked like Nosferatu: dressed in black, a thin long face, widow's peak, and he spoke in the most convoluted way about structure and so on. Lecek's favourite phrase was 'The dramaticalogical construction requires that...' He prefaced everything with it. Then, after first drafts were in, the Polish people decided they wanted more of their Polish myths and legends in it.

Paul Davies: Which you knew a lot about of course ...

Mark Shirrefs: [laughs] Yes. So we asked them if they could give us some examples of their 'myths and legends' to work on. And there's silence. Then after conferring they said: 'We'll send you some'. So John and I go back to Australia and we're waiting and waiting, and nothing comes, so we go to the state library and find some Polish myths and legends and started incorporating them into the story. Then some weeks later a package arrives from Poland and it's a book of Polish myths and legends—in Polish—and a letter saying, 'We're sure you'll have no trouble having these translated'. As it happened, the woman at John's local laundromat was Polish, and she was able to explain them. But they were legends we had found anyway. So juggling those sorts of issues is the most difficult part of it.

Paul Davies: Aside from Lecek's concerns, how important is structure in any script? Are there rules to be followed?

Mark Shirrefs: The problem with Australian television is probably mostly in the storytelling aspect. I discovered this working as a script producer on *Pig's Breakfast*.

Pigs Breakfast (1999 – 2000)

Mark Shirrefs: A lot of commercial television writers have a real problem with story. My theory is that series and serial television provides writers with such worked out storylines that all they have to do is basically paint by numbers. And they don't get the sense of what it really means to tell a story. It's the Scene Breakdown stage where you discover things haven't been worked out from the Storyline.

Paul Davies: That's where the structural problems emerge?

Mark Shirrefs: Yes. And you expect the writers to work out those things for themselves. Or at least ring up and talk about it. But we found they just weren't dealing with this problem. Either they thought it was just kid's TV and it didn't matter—which is an appalling attitude—or it's a much bigger issue about telling a story.

Paul Davies: Is the spoon feeding itself part of the problem, the fact that writers aren't given due importance, that the basic principles of writing are being lost?

Mark Shirrefs: It's a complex question. But I often find the narrative drive is missing, the things that actually keep an audience glued to the screen. The stakes in a story often aren't high enough. I would like to see writers given the opportunity to create stories which can embrace those things and aren't interfered with by story departments. But John and I have devised all our own material so we've had a lot of freedom. Nobody else edits our work. We get feedback from producers and directors, of course. But when you've got good quality control over your scripts, then the product will speak for itself. Certainly I think long running television shows are a bad idea. You just get more of the same. Even on shorter series there's a burn out factor. The trouble is the opportunities on Australian TV are really limited and when those opportunities are taken up by long running shows, that means we really lack a lot of variety. The diversity of expression just doesn't happen.

Paul Davies: Does that indicate a kind of 'If it ain't broke don't fix it' approach from the Networks?

Mark Shirrefs: It's certainly much easier not to take risks. The ratings are all-important. But there is also evidence that Australians like to see Australians on television. Which is why a lot of those shows that you've worked on—*Homicide* and *Stingers* and so on—have all been so successful. But at the same time we get cops and hospital shows from the UK and America with more resources. The trick with long running series is to make them fresh. I believe we have a unique vision of the world in Australia and it's one of the reasons why our children's TV works so well overseas.

Paul Davies: It's really the unsung success story, isn't it, the success of Australian kids TV against a lot of odds?

Mark Shirrefs: Absolutely. The Oriental Pearl television tower in Shanghai is the third tallest man made structure in the world. It has an audience footprint of 200 million people. Whenever Heather Mitchell [the villain in the two *Spellbinder* series] went overseas she was mobbed by kids. Likewise the Polish actor who played the wise old *Spellbinder*. Children's television is the best returning investment the FFC have made by far.

Spellbinder (1995)
A prank gone wrong sends 15 year old Paul Reynolds
into an alternate dimension

Paul Davies: Is there a different obligation when you're writing for kids? Special parameters?

Mark Shirrefs: Kids TV is regulated by the ABA (Australian Broadcasting Authority). There are guidelines that you have to adhere to. But the interesting thing about the guidelines is that they are very positive and do all the things that point you in the direction of making a really good story. Positive role models, not about violence ...

Paul Davies: Something adult drama could learn from?

Mark Shirrefs: What children's television does is encourage really good values in people—the use of imagination, working together rather than in opposition—not to the exclusion of conflict and drama of course. But the other thing is, it's actually there to stimulate kids' imaginations and adult television almost seems to do the opposite. The things I remember watching as a kid were *The Outer Limits*, *The Twilight Zone*, those programmes about places I'd never been ... and that's what lead me to the fantasy stuff. Fantasy doesn't have to be aliens and monsters. Look at the UK series, *Cold Feet*, for example. All of a sudden you're out of the ordinary and you see things in a different way. And as programme creators, we have that responsibility to our viewers to reflect back not just what they know anyway, but something else—a different way of looking at things.

Paul Davies: How does the collaboration with John Thomson work in practice?

Mark Shirrefs: We have a number of ways of working. We get together in the first instance and do the concepts, work out the bible together. We spend a lot of time developing the stories. Most of the work is in the transition from concept to storyline to scene breakdown, especially in terms of getting the structure right, the hooks and so on. And then we can go off and write drafts individually. Sometimes, if it's difficult, each of us will write the same thing and see what we end up with. And sometimes one of us will have a nice slant on the scene or the other person will have written some good dialogue... or in the worst situation, both of us have written something we each really like and we have to decide which one to go with.

Paul Davies: Do you call in a referee?

Mark Shirrefs: [laughs] We haven't had to yet. It's a good process.

Paul Davies: What are you looking for as an editor when you edit John's scripts and he edits yours?

Mark Shirrefs: A good editor needs to know what makes a good story, particularly about structure. As script producer on *Pig's Breakfast*, my job was to commission the writers, talk them through the storylines, edit the first drafts and then take their second drafts, give them a bit of feedback, let them do a polish and then do the final [shooting] draft myself. Assuming things go well, it's just cosmetic changes at that stage and throwing in the odd joke here and there. But in the worst cases—more often than I would have liked—I had to rewrite scripts completely, which is a sobering experience. But as far as editing goes, you need to sit above it, which is hard sometimes. This is where a knowledge of the craft elements of scriptwriting are important. There are a number of good books—Syd Field, Robert McKee, Linda Aronson... And you need to absorb all that stuff, even if you don't do it formally through a screenwriting course. The series we're doing at the moment [another co-production with Chinese Television] is a thirteen parter and what's good about that is you don't have to stretch the story so far. Thirteen half hours allows you to tell a story with really good character interaction. It's closer to doing a feature film, like a mini-series almost. It allows you to think about telling stories with images.

Paul Davies: Is that a piece of advice you give your students? Emphasise the visual?

Mark Shirrefs: There was a programme about the human body on TV recently which dealt with the mind, and there's this thing called the 'Mental Olympics'. One of the tests is to remember the sequence of a pack of cards. The guy who's won three years in a row does it by assigning each card a quality or a character. So the card 7 equals '007', for example, and then he makes up a story about them. That's how he remembers the sequence. People had vision before they had language and I think we're still primarily a visually oriented culture. Obviously words are incredibly important. But the things that stick with you after seeing a film aren't necessarily the exchanges of dialogue, but the images that convey the information. In my teaching I use images from *Apocalypse Now*—some of the most extraordinary on celluloid—as an example of imagery in storytelling.

Paul Davies: Are camera directions important in the script?

Mark Shirrefs: Most directors tend to ignore them. When I write a script, I want it to be a good read. And if you write camera directions it takes readers out of the story. If you write it cleverly enough, the director almost has no choice but to shoot it in the way you've intended. So you can insinuate camera directions without actually spelling it out. That's an acting technique too, of course. One of things you're taught as an actor is to examine the image behind the line. So an acting approach is to take each line apart and give it an image, and analyse how that makes you feel emotionally. It's the same with a writer. A writer has to know at every point in the script what is actually on the screen. The scenes I can see the easiest are very easy to write. I'm just translating. The difficult ones are the ones where I can't see what's happening, and they require several attempts to get it right. Often, you look back at something on the page and realise you can cut away all this dross and just get to the essence of it and make that clearer. And whether you're aware of it or not, your subconscious writer has put what you really want in the scene, but it just isn't clear enough. It's like sculpting. You cut away all the pieces that aren't the sculpture. A first draft is like being in the coal mine. You work really hard to dig it out. You're dealing for the first time with what people say to each other and how they say it. You start to find the comedy. The second draft is much easier and you can have more fun.

Paul Davies: Film or TV: is there a difference for the scriptwriter?

Mark Shirrefs: Writing for television is much harder than film because there's less money to do more. And if you want an audience to watch it, it has to be really good, because they can just get up and leave the room. People have paid money in the cinema and are less likely to walk. There are also more options on the box. A big movie could be on the other channel or the tennis—things that go for hours. It's much harder. So you have to be more creative. And in fact the only way to have a career in Australia is to write television. You can actually make a living.

Paul Davies: Are agents important for getting work?

Mark Shirrefs: We got an agent after we won an AWGIE for *The Girl From Tomorrow*. It was good, because it made us feel somebody wanted us. They negotiated a couple of contracts for us, which was fine, but they didn't help much finding work because basically John and I create our own. We decided eventually that we could employ a lawyer to do the contracts, so we parted ways amicably with the agents. And in fact they said, 'We're surprised you stayed with us so long'. Now we do the negotiating ourselves.

Paul Davies: Do you have an average working day?

Mark Shirrefs: I have an office I go to every day. I did write the second series of *Girl From Tomorrow* in the second bedroom in my flat, which meant I could work till 2am without having to go home. And my partner Diana was very impressed that I'd put on an ironed shirt and go into the bedroom to work. But it became a trap because I could never get away from it. If I have a problem—I don't call it a block—I'll do the accounts, or go see a movie or go to the gym, which is really good because it's like meditation, it clears your mind. I'll sit on the exercise bike and a solution will pop up. You need to have a number of different strategies of attacking your work. It gets easier with experience. Plus the mind is like a flywheel. It takes a lot of effort to get it moving, but once it's up and running—like on *Pig's Breakfast*—it's like a juggernaut and anything that gets in its way is crushed beneath it. [laughs]

Paul Davies: What advice would you give to writers starting out now?

Mark Shirrefs: Write what you know. It means that you have a starting point. If you can see some situation in your own life that makes you feel something ... It's what I find so difficult to convey to my students sometimes, that the only time a story is truly vivid is when it has a strong emotional spine. People like the story of how the boy gets from being dumped in the forest to back home. What they're really interested in there is the emotional logic of survival. What does it mean for this boy to be put through all this?

Paul Davies: So there's a mechanical structure ...

Mark Shirrefs: Yes, the craft element, the Syd Field aspect.

Paul Davies: Then there's an emotional structure that's separate and different from that?

Mark Shirrefs: Yes, and the 'how to' books don't often deal with it. This is where 'the stakes' come in. What are the stakes in any given story? Mostly it's life and death stakes. Is the character going to physically survive this experience? But equally important is the character's emotional journey—how will they survive emotionally and psychologically?

Paul Davies: Is Reality TV a threat to the role of the writer?

Mark Shirrefs: I don't think so at all. We'll get bored with it pretty soon. It's like *Gilligan's Island* without the jokes. There's a novelty element to it. But stories have a vital role to play in our society. We live in a time of such rapid change that the things that once held a society together become more tenuous. And we consume so many stories. People are reading more books than ever, for example.

Paul Davies: Plus the average number of movies one would see in a lifetime ...

Mark Shirrefs: Yes, huge. But stories always occur in everything. We're always looking for them because it's a way that we learn. Stories convey information to people about how to cope with different situations. The Reality TV stuff doesn't seem to provide any level of insight.

Paul Davies: It's also based on some pretty negative impulses—like greed, eviction, ganging up.

Mark Shirrefs: Yes, we'll get bored with it quickly and we'll go back to the things that have always sustained human society, which is people getting together and telling stories. Humans are also fascinated by patterns. When somebody dies, we want to know why that happened. We're looking for a pattern to give us a sense of security. And that comes from when we were hunters—us versus the natural world. We're looking at a patch of jungle. And it's green, green, yellow, green. And its—oops, yellow is the colour of lion fur! So we look at the pattern and we look at the disruption in the pattern and that disruption is a piece of information that is extremely useful to us. I think a story is a pattern with a disruption in it. And what we're interested in seeing is whether that disruption destroys the pattern of the story so that it never quite gets back together again. And by the end of the story, there's always another pattern created out of what's just happened. But above all, stories give us coping skills, like the narrative cure that some psychologists use. What it does is help people make sense of something—their trauma, grief and so on. It gives them a pattern they can understand. So by writing a story, you confront the issues of who you are or who the character is. It's a powerful tool.

Mark Shirrefs with the cast of *Storming St. Kilda By Tram*
which he directed in (1988)

"What children's television does is encourage really good values in people—the use of imagination, working together rather than in opposition—it's actually there to stimulate kids' imaginations and adult television almost seems to do the opposite."

Interview held at the Dogs Bar, Acland Street St. Kilda.

GETTING TO THE HEART OF THE MATTER
Andrew Knight
METRO #139 (2003)

In his own words, Andrew Knight has created "some of Australia's highest rating television series and some of its worst." Together with Deb Cox he wrote the acclaimed series *Seachange* and *After The Deluge.* Prior to this Andrew "held the pen" in rooms full of very talented comic actors on shows such as *Fast Forward, The D Generation,* and *Full Frontal.* Other credits include *Spotswood, Kangaroo Palace* and *The Fast Lane* (co-written with John Clarke. His most recent work with Deb Cox is *CrashBurn,* a 13 part series commissioned by Sue Masters for Network Ten.

Paul Davies: You spoke yesterday on the session about 'Character' (at the Byron Writers' Festival 2003) about one of the problems of Australian television drama being the shoe-horning of characters into formulas and structures that are already developed and one of the great revolutions of *Seachange* is that it breaks away from that.

Andrew Knight: Even more so in the new series *Crash Burn.* It's largely a necessity.

Paul Davies: Yes. Because even with something like *Seachange* a major set is the magistrate's court and there's two cops and a pub...and some episodes hang on the idea of a crime or misdemeanour. So it's still the story of a magistrate.

Sigrid Thornton and William McInnes
Seachange (1998 – 2000)

Andrew Knight: Deb (Cox) never wanted to make it a magistrate that was my idea. But to me there are so many different restrictions when you do a television series and there's this necessity that you do have a limited number of sets and limited number of locations. There are a whole lot of parameters and you do need to confine story. What we tried to do with the magistrate thing was turn it on its head and never use it at the centre of the story. And we'd try to make it allude to the philosophical point we were trying to make in every episode. So occasionally it worked and occasionally it didn't. But when you've got a very long series with many writers it causes stasis. You have to do it as a McDonalds. You have to say this character does this. Otherwise a writer will go away and do it in any way that feels comfortable. And a lot of the job of script editors on series is to bring them into line. The great joy of writing with Deb is we are our own editors and so we can make our characters shift.

Paul Davies: An unheard of freedom.

Andrew Knight: It is but it will catch up with us if we have too many failures…

Paul Davies: No danger of that yet.

Andrew Knight: Oh I don't know…*After the Deluge* didn't rate. It got great reviews.

David Wenham, Rachel Griffiths, Hugo Weaving, Samuel Johnson
After the Deluge (2003)

Paul Davies: Was that because it was on Channel 10 ?

Andrew Knight: I think it was hard for the standard Cox/Knight audience to locate us there.

Paul Davies: And equally so for the Channel 10 audience...

Andrew Knight: Yeah I think they had trouble finding how you connect with an audience that isn't *Big Brother.* I admire 10 for trying.

Paul Davies: Is that Sue Masters?

Andrew Knight: Yes. Originally we were going to do it at the ABC but it was in the Shier era. And it was a bit of a nightmare. And given that the ABC is on such a tight budget it would have been almost impossible to finance. We might have got there but we would never have got that cast. That cast was an extra million dollars on top of the whole production. So there was a thrill to have the appropriate amount of money to make it for a change. I'm not having a go at the ABC I just wish they could get more money.

Paul Davies: But also mini series seem to go in and out of fashion all the time. Writer's love them because you can have that expression.

Andrew Knight: They're kind of easier. The thing about them too is, unlike film, you've got a chance to follow multiple strands. In fact you have to have a kind of Victorian structure to it (like a Dickens novel).

Paul Davies: Which were serialized in magazines anyway.

Andrew Knight: Yes. You have a bit here and a bit there. Series has got that but because of the implicit production problems you always feel caged. We had real troubles with *Crash Burn*. We'd say we want a traveling shot - no you can't have a traveling shot - okay, so we say we'll do it on a phone…yes okay do it on a phone, but not in that set…So series are very frustrating things to do in this country. It's not anyone's fault. It's just that the budgets are so frigging tight.

Paul Davies: On a *Blue Heelers* once we had to get the TAC to sponsor a car crash, so long as we gave them a story about old people giving up their licences.

Andrew Knight: You can see why product placement would be so attractive.

Paul Davies: Perhaps it could fund the shortfalls.

Andrew Knight: Something has to. Something has to give. We just can't afford to fund drama at the current level. On series production there's not much leeway, you've usually given away most of your back end just to make the production in the first place. You're fees aren't all that enormously high. And might have to sustain you across a four year period.

Paul Davies: Unless there's the overseas sale…

Andrew Knight: But even then very little will come back because usually you've relinquished those rights just to get it financed in the first place. Either there's been a distribution guarantee or you've pre-sold your biggest market just to get there. Like if you've pre-sold England, you're getting cable and distribution and if they're taking 35% out of it, there ain't nothing coming back. My money comes from making high turn over television.

Paul Davies: So you started with comedy, *Fast Forward*, *D Gen*, *Full Frontal* period. You say you wrote jokes because it pulled chicks. (laughter)

Andrew Knight: It didn't actually. It was an attempt to.

Paul Davies: So there's now there's the more serious stuff. *After The Deluge*. I'm not sure about *Crash Burn*…

Crash Burn (2003)
Catherine McClements Aaron Blaby

Andrew Knight: *Crash Burn* is a fusion of both.

Paul Davies: And even *Seachange* has it's moments of seriousness…

Andrew Knight: *Seachange* had some high drama. I just don't see life in Macbethian terms. It's not all gloom and doom.

Paul Davies: But *After The Deluge* certainly is the most sober work…

Andrew Knight: And it got a great reaction. John Clark once said to me it's a bad idea to tell people you're making a comedy. That's sort of how I feel about it. When you're inside the material it just dictates what you're going to do anyway. If I seen an opportunity to be funny I'll be funny. I don't set out slavishly to do jokes or anything.

Paul Davies: But watching you here at the writers festival…there's a lot of laughs in the tent when you're on.

Andrew Knight: I just get kind of bored. If I think I've got nothing particular to offer the universe here. I'll just tell a joke.

Paul Davies: Which people love of course. And anyway there's always a point under the joke…

Andrew Knight: When you look at Peter Cook and Dudley Moore who, along with Humphries, were my heroes. All of a sudden they changed the nature of what you could say. And they did it by giving licence to laugh at it. If you give people that licence then you can actually discuss it seriously. And I also think there's very few writers that have the gravitas to be serious all the time. After Shakespeare, Tolstoy and few others it's pretty hard to do that. My insights are less insightful and more just durr...The good thing about working with Deb is that you've got two brains trying to extract where the core of an idea is. She was so useful on *After The Deluge*.

Paul Davies: Was she a co-writer on that?

Andrew Knight: She was the script editor. And because I've worked with Deb for so long her function went way beyond that. I was the writer but there's whole passages that just sound and look like Deb for me. And she was just very gracious in that. She dragged it all out of me.

Paul Davies: You've obviously had a very successful creative partnership with Deb and you spoke here about how in *Seachange* she would adopt certain characters and you'd adopt others. The male/female roles are an obvious starting point but did it reverse itself as well? She'd write a male part and you the female?

Andrew Knight: Oh yes. We've just written *Crash Burn* which is two, twinned half-hours where one follows a male and one follows a female - with lots of crossovers. Two half hours with completely contained stories, on the same night side by side except when you put them together you say Oh - the story was different. Oh I missed that and then that happened.

Paul Davies: In the 'Getting Personal' session at the Festival you were saying that the nature of 'truth' is a malleable thing.

Andrew Knight: And I think the more eloquent you are the more you can distort it. Language is the great tool of obfuscation.

Paul Davies: There's the writer character in a Dutch film called *The Fourth Man* who's giving a lecture and what he says about himself is that a writer 'lies the truth.'

Andrew Knight: Yes.

Paul Davies: In terms of your working methodology. When you come to a project you say you start from the flaws in the characters and chisel back through that to what they're really on about. And that's what drives the story.

Andrew Knight: Yes.

Paul Davies: So, before *Seachange* you're running this comedy business (Artist Services with Steve Vizard), you're keeping hundreds of people employed so much so that you're almost crying as you write sketches...and then comes *Seachange*. You've probably been asked a 1000

times but was there a personal 'seachange' for you in going from the sketches to the drama series?

Andrew Knight: It was strange. Most people interpreted it literally. Tim Winton has been getting stuck into us. He hated the series because he said it wasn't true. And I probably agree with him on a lot of levels. But it wasn't about dropping out. It was more about the need for a community. The need for a connection. And that was something I could respond to when I was writing it under great pressure in a room in the city. While Deb was living up here (in Byron Bay).

Paul Davies: But you come here, too. And a lot of people come to Byron with the same sort of agenda. The healing, searching for another way...a sense of community.

Andrew Knight: I do think there's something about being in contact with the natural world. It's healing. But I do think it's really rather a limited idea to say I'm dropping out. I've just got to find myself. You'll just find tedium.

Paul Davies: Well one local legend has it that if you come here to be healed you'd better move on when you are or you'll get sick all over again.

Andrew Knight: That's fantastic. I think that's exactly true. You have to have some sense of forward movement. I think it's fine to come up here and run a business but I also run into a lot of deeply depressed people who just don't know what they're doing.

Paul Davies: At the end of series 3 of *Seachange* you decide to pull the plug. It must have been one of the more interesting decisions in Australian television. The series is so popular, it hits the national pulse, it's got half the country watching, striving for a better way, something the city can't provide... But then you and Deb so no, that's it. Against all this pressure to keep going...

Andrew Knight: It wasn't quite as much pressure as you might think. At the time at the ABC - I have to keep saying that "at the time" (the Shier period) Sue Masters had just left and she was the greatest advocate for the show. The ABC hierarchy at that time many of whom waved at the crowd later and said yeah, that was us, thank you we did it, we made *Seachange* - they didn't really actually want it at the start. But Deb and I just decided we didn't want to go on with it. For the very reason we're talking about - we're just going to repeat ourselves here. And I thought we were getting a bit too baroque at the end anyway with the plots...

Paul Davies: The tunnel story?

Andrew Knight: Yeah, I don't know what I was thinking ...

Paul Davies: You were looking for a bridge to somewhere else. A way out perhaps? (laughter)

Andrew Knight: Yeah. I think I was wanting it to talk about bigger themes and yet it (Seachange) didn't have a chassis that could contain it. And I just like to get out of things before I repeat myself. Because I did so much sketch comedy, I've got this inner thing that just tells me I can't do any more of this - so I get out - probably prematurely.

Paul Davies: So you leave them wanting more.

Andrew Knight: Yeah. And we did. And when we finished, most papers in the country had us on the front page saying 'last episode tonight.' It was kind of a strange phenomenon. The whole thing. So we got out and we felt some kind of dignity in that. I just wish the last episode had been good…(laughs)

Paul Davies: But you're very modest about things generally. I kept hearing you mention the failures here at the festival. Is that some sort of self deprecating thing?

Andrew Knight: I know that I've had a lot of success. But I'm also conscious that I stiffed out a lot too. And I'm from a well mannered family. You don't talk about yourself much. John Clark had warned me that interviews were a nightmare. You also get asked questions about which you have no opinion and you fill in the gap. And it is often wrong. I also like to tell young writers it's perfectly legitimate to fuck up and fuck up a lot. It's part of the process.

Paul Davies: So only being as good as your last show doesn't apply.

Andrew Knight: I don't believe that actually. I hope not. You've got to remember Shakespeare wrote *Troilus and Cressida.* For godsake. Even the greatest can just step out.

Paul Davies: Not to mention *Titus Andronicus*

Andrew Knight: *Titus Andronicus* (laughs) even worse. I mean what was he thinking! But you don't look at a body of work and go. Ah, *Henry IV* Part - whatever … that was a flop wasn't it? You look at the whole thing. You have to look at the body of work. I think this country has a kind of messianic view of new talent - and I'm all for getting new people and giving them a big break. But I'm more interested in their body of work at the end. That's why I gravitate towards writers who've done it a lot and pulled it off a lot. I love musicians who grow old with grace. Paul Simon, Tom Waits…

Paul Davies: You were also saying in the 'Getting Personal' session how their music was more moving for some of your writing students than a scene from a TV drama where a man watches the death of his daughter.

Andrew Knight: I keep saying you've got to give people a licence to feel.

Paul Davies: After *Crash Burn?*

Andrew Knight: I don't know. I really don't. I think the network want another series but I don't know how sustainable it is. I loved doing *After the Deluge*. I loved having a big project that I could spend some time on and do the way that I wanted to.

Paul Davies: And despite your denials perhaps based or grounded in very personal experiences.

Andrew Knight: Oh yeah. I think a lot of why you write is to put closure on it yourself. To give yourself resolutions that don't happen in real life. I think its one of the great privileges of writing. You can have a resolution.

Paul Davies: But you've also managed to create an opportunity for Australian television to be more personal. To get beyond the cop-show/doctor-show formulas.

Andrew Knight: I did a series with John Clark in 1985 called *The Fast Lane* and it was uneven and it was patchy. We got lots wrong but I think if people were to look at the scripts they would notice that that's what we were doing then. And when I say John Clark and I - I was his apprentice really. But what we were trying to do was re-define the way it worked. And if that series had worked I think we would have seen more change coming. It was about marrying comedy and drama and not telling people what was what and exploring themes and taking philosophical positions…I found sketch comedy very useful for defining where a character is and making sure they had different voices. A good sketch will go quickly to the heart of the matter.

Paul Davies: There was an ensemble feel about it. You were working with great talent.

Andrew Knight: I've claimed way too much credit for that series. I look at the talent in that show… I just happened to be in the room at the time taking notes. You get someone like a Jane (Turner) or a Gina (Riley) or a Magda (Szbanski) and you get a pen. What I used to do was edit, harness and tie it together. I'd love to work with Ted Emery again – if you're asking me what I'd like to do. To do a comedy with him. I know Ted would love to direct drama. But why bother… He's the cleverest comedy director in the country. He defined how it should happen. Up to that time it was, you know, someone who had covered sport would come in. He was a man with this constant humour. It couldn't have worked without him. There's also Andrea Denholm who's the one with the motor skills. She's an ex-lawyer and a producer and she's a writer. So she's absolutely perfect complement to us. So we're probably going to call the company now Cox Denholm Knight. Sounds more like a law firm. She's been an absolute blessing. One of those people who just gets the detail. Who's got enough creative sensibility to know when to come in. She knows how hard it is to write something. When to put pressure on. When not to.

Paul Davies: How hard is it to bring in other writers?

Andrew Knight: Very hard. We've got a bad reputation.

Paul Davies: You haven't appeared on the Writer's Guild blacklist yet.

Andrew Knight: No but we probably will. And some of it is deserved because the sort of stuff we're doing doesn't have too many precedents in this country. So when you're writing we're working in a Darwinian slime there. We had so much trouble on *Crash Burn* because we hadn't really pinned it down. We had good writers who tried very hard and we tried very hard and spent all our writing money and the scripts didn't work so we had to go back and do the whole series using some of the material. They were great writers but we hadn't established it in our own head. What it was all about.

Paul Davies: It's hard for other writers until something goes to air…

Andrew Knight: Yeah, and you think you can write. I think I could write an episode of *The Sopranos* but I probably couldn't. But I look at it and I think yeah, I know these characters but when you get to write it - it's very different. I'm a terrible editor. I just want to pick up the pen and change it. And writers hate that.

Paul Davies: The role of the editor as it's changing is increasingly becoming more a negotiator/diplomat pulling in all the network feedback and the producer/director feedback back to the writer - a clearing house rather than a creative thing…

Andrew Knight: That's why I don't like series. There's too many people involved. And sketch comedy too. We'd have 150 sketches each week, you'd end up shooting 40 of them. And most of my job was saying 'no'. You didn't have time to say think about this or that's not right… You're under so much pressure you just say: "it's not funny." Which is a fairly fatuous remark because it might be funny to someone else. But it's why Deb and I just wanted to work together. There were some great writing experiences on *Seachange* with Hannie (Rayson) and Andrea (Denholm) and with Max (Dan) and that was just a joy because they were people I'd known for a long time… it was fun, but *Crash Burn* was a lot harder because it was so complex.

(Interview conducted at the Byron Writers Festival, Sunday 3 August 2003)

SEARCHING FOR THE STORY ENGINE
Roger Simpson
METRO #135 (2003)

"I love analysing what the story engine is going to be
and putting your finger on it."

**Paul Davies: Just to get some background, Roger, you trained as a solicitor
and came from New Zealand to work at Crawfords?**

Roger Simpson: I came from New Zealand to be a writer. Optimistically and
naively to tell a series about the mining industry which had just crashed.
'Poseidon' and all that. Scandal. And I naively thought because it was
newsworthy there would also be good drama. But I was wrong. (laughs) The
whole industry laid a very big smell and the last thing anyone wanted to talk
about was something that bad.

Paul Davies: There was a film called the Nickel Queen...

Roger Simpson: Yes. And I think that suffered a similar fate. That was at least
an attempt at a comedy, mine was a serious drama.

Paul Davies: And a series?

Roger Simpson: Yes.

Paul Davies: So you went straight for television, rather than film?

Roger Simpson: Yes. I'd worked as a barrister and solicitor for three years and I was working part time in TV in New Zealand as a comedy writer, writing gags for a variety show. But New Zealand only did 8 hours of drama a year and they shared that between 8 writers, so you couldn't make a living out of it. Being a writer in New Zealand then was a part time job. So I came to Australia to flog off this series called "The "Investors" -about the mining industry - on my way to England because my dream was to write Z Cars. (laughs) A long time ago. But I never got there because I ran out of money in Sydney...

Paul Davies: So like a lot of New Zealanders you turned to crime...

Roger Simpson: (laughs) I turned to crime. Hector Crawford threw me a liferaft. I'd been in Australia for a year running out of options and was just about to go back over the Tasman to be a barrister for the rest of my life and Hector was running a two week course for new writers, because he was expanding at the time. In 1971 he had *Division 4, Homicide, Matlock Police* and *Solo One*. Four shows on four networks and he was running short of writers. So he ran a seminar for people interested in writing drama. I wrongly thought I knew how to write drama because I'd written some in New Zealand... But 4 of us survived that seminar and are still around today. Peter Shreck, Vince Moran...

Paul Davies: ... Peter Shreck is currently story producing Young Lions...

Roger Simpson: Yes. And Vince Moran retired a few years ago. And Patrick Edgeworth and me - we were the four survivors out of a course of about 14 people.

Paul Davies: Was Dorothy Crawford involved in that?

Roger Simpson: Yes. And Ian Jones and Terry Stapleton. And Tom Hegarty. They were all our teachers. It was the sort of thing that doesn't happen any more because it was an all in-house writing system - as you know. In those days freelancers didn't exist. There were the odd few who worked for the ABC. But basically the Crawford system was inhouse so you became a staff writer. You were rated like journalists. You started as C and worked up to B, A.

Paul Davies: So there was actually a term - A writer, B writer and so on...

Roger Simpson: Yes. It was to do with money. Rated like journalists.

Paul Davies: In fact a lot of early Crawford writers were ex-journalists - being the only professional writers around?

Roger Simpson: Yes. No film schools. Nothing like that. So I started the same week that Roger le Measurier did. He didn't go to the seminar because he wanted to be a script editor. So he got a job as a trainee script editor.

Paul Davies: Did he edit your scripts?

Roger Simpson: He did on *Division four*. But after that Roger went overseas and travelled and we didn't actually get together until 1981, ten years later. He was always more frivolous than I. (laughs). He sensibly toured around the world and had a good time.

Paul Davies: So - two and a half years at Crawfords as a staff writer and then what?

Roger Simpson: I was one of the writers who went out into the big bad world. There were a few freelancers like Tony Morphett and Colin Free, a few established, older writers. But not many of us youngsters. That was another difficult transition because I thought I had *Division 4*s and *Homicide*s sorted. But it evaporated quickly because Crawfords wanted people inhouse and didn't want to encourage free lancers. But luckily *Power Without Glory* (based on the novel by Frank Hardy) came along on the ABC so I got a gig there and that was the start of my freelance career really.

Power Without Glory (1976)

Roger Simpson: Then, *I Can Jump Puddles*. A one-off called *The Trial of Ned Kelly* where I did a courtroom 90 minuter. I tried to prove Kelly was guilty of manslaughter not murder. Tried to get him off. It had a narrator who went around interrupting people.

Paul Davies: Like *Consider Your Verdict*?

Roger Simpson: It was a bit more adventurous than that. I wouldn't call it a big success for the ABC. It was a wee bit ambitious for itself. But it's all experience.

Paul Davies: Is *Squizzy Taylor* the first big project you do with Roger?

Roger Simpson: Yes. But before that I had a period of going back to New Zealand - still living in Australia. But New Zealand got a new head of drama called John McRae. He reckoned the way New Zealand could get ahead in the world was not to compete with adult drama because the English and Americans did it too well. But to be able to find a niche in children's drama and he put all his budget into really well resourced kids' series. And I did four of those over the next six years. And when they had trouble getting a producer for the second one, Le Measurier had come back from overseas, and I said it's time, Roger, for you to be a producer. (laughs). He said I don't know anything about being a producer I've just learnt script editing. So I said there's not a lot of difference (laughs). Just a bit of casting and a bit of budgetary control, you can do it. The New Zealanders are desperate. So Roger went over and he produced two of them. I was still living here. This was just a job.

Paul Davies: So this is the late 70s now ?

Roger Simpson: Yes, and then towards the end of the 70s we started talking about setting up this movie. But it took 2 years. So it was 1981 before *Squizzy Taylor* happened. That's where it started and Simpson Le Measurier have just had our 21st year.

Squizzy Taylor (1982)

Paul Davies: After *Squizzy Taylor*?

Roger Simpson: Nothing for three years.

Paul Davies: A deafening silence. The phone stopped ringing...

Roger Simpson: Again its the naivety of the young writer. Thinking all he had to do was make a film and then your career looks after itself. It's a smash hit. You're asked to go to Hollywood. But of course the reality is: it ran for 8 weeks. Made a box office smash in Australia. It's still in video shops. But we weren't ready for it. We hadn't even written another script. I don't know what we thought was going to happen. So Roger went back to work as a free lance script editor and I went back writing television. But we kept the partnership. And we spent three years of pitching in all directions- films TV series, kids' shows. Everything. And we finally got a gig where we made *Sword of Honour* which was a mini series about the Vietnam War.

Sword of Honour 1986

Paul Davies: Which was very highly regarded, still...

Roger Simpson: I think we got our first Logie with that. And that did make a difference. *Squizzy Taylor* we didn't get noticed. Though it opened the Sydney film festival. But that's about all it did. At least it didn't close it.

Paul Davies: Was it a 10BA film?

Roger Simpson: Yes 10BA was invented about the time we were trying to get it up. *Sword of Honour* was a 10BA project too. As was our next mini series *Nancy Wake*. So we had a 10BA phase.

Paul Davies: Is *Skirts* the next cab off the rank ?

Roger Simpson: Before *Skirts* was *Darlings of the Gods*, a co-production with Thames Television. Mini series started to sell. The era of the Mini Series. Funded by 10BA. It was fantastic. They were big budget, the poms liked the production values. And were buying them. Australian Television got a very high profile very quickly. And this project with Thames was at the height of that boom.

Paul Davies: This is the early 80s now.

Roger Simpson: Yes. Then it all went bang. It imploded on itself and politicians said there's too much tax avoidance money going into film and television. And like all booms there came a crunch. That's when we did *Skirts*. Which was our first television drama series not funded or subsidised by 10BA.

Kate Gillick and Antoinette Byron in *Skirts*

Paul Davies: This was for channel 7?

Roger Simpson: The famous story about that is that they required a gritty 8.30 police drama about a community policing squad. But after we'd made the first half of the first series they decided to put it on at 7.30 on Sunday night after Disneyland, with the instruction to hang on to the same audience. We said how do we do that with a gritty police show? Well - start changing the scripts. So the first 11 went to air as gritty police drama then the programmers panicked and put it to a 9.30 show just as the soft scripts came through. (laughs). They'd been advertising this hard edged show....

Paul Davies: This is reminiscent of the *Something In the Air* story. Do you despair sometimes at the way programmers treat what you give them?

Roger Simpson: It's very hard. They sort of, on one hand, understand the process and that it takes time. Scripts are written a long way ahead and it takes time and it is what it is. And it's very hard to change quickly. You can change it from series to series but it's very had to change it on the way through. But even with that knowledge they get stuck with their schedule. And if it isn't working in the schedule they panic. They shift their cards around.

Paul Davies: Is it a failure of nerve on their part? Not to trust what you give them? Or are they bound by ratings so much...

Roger Simpson: They're under so much pressure to succeed in ratings and they've got advertisers screaming at them too of course..

Paul Davies: You'd think that it would be different with the ABC...

RS Yes you would. It was our blackest time. The Jonathan Shier years were the worst. We've been through some rough times. But nothing like that. To see a national broadcaster enfeebled in that way... it's just appalling.

Paul Davies: *Halifax* was another SLM success story. Twenty one telemovies in all...

Rebecca Gibney, Hugo Weaving *Halifax FP* (1994 – 2002)

Roger Simpson: Yes. Roger and I have kept ourselves adaptable. Because the rules change. 10BA is there one minute then its gone the next. Video tape drama becomes the thing to do then suddenly there's a swing against that. *Halifax* became a creature of FFC subsidised drama. We made *Snowy* as a thirteen part mini-series before we made *Halifax*. But then, when too many 13 part mini-series came along, the FFC started running out of dough, so they had to change the rules. And they favoured telemovies. So there was *Feds*, *Cody*, *Singapore Sling*, and *Halifax*. And *Halifax* was the survivor.

Paul Davies: When you say "*Snowy*", that's "*Snowy* -the shovel" (not *The Man From Snowy River*)

Roger Simpson: Yes. We had big plans for "*Snowy* -the shovel", it was going to be a series of 13-part series. Series one was the immigrants arriving, Australia after the war, and the beginning of the Snowy (River Scheme). And Series two was going to be about the tunnel and Series 3 was going to the consummation of the scheme, twenty, thirty years on. But they changed the rules.

Paul Davies: So only the first series got in the can?

Roger Simpson: Also the ratings were spectacular when it went out. But every week it went down a bit. Because it was a serial. And Channel 9 panicked because they said it was a great idea, but people tend to feel they've missed a few episodes. There's no point in joining it late - which wasn't true. But that was the perception. They were ratings you'd die for now. High 30s. Only the Brownlow medal count and the Eurovision song contest gets higher these days. (laughs)

Paul Davies: That remains an issue though now with something like *Stingers*, were you are getting large narrative arcs spread over sometimes 5 or more episodes. So the story department problem becomes how to give each episode enough self containment to be viewable alone and still connect to the stories on either side.

Peter Phelps, Gary Sweet *Stingers* (1998 – 2004)

Roger Simpson: It's an ongoing issue. And the networks are always turning the tap on and off as far as the serial aspects of a series are concerned. The story department on *Stringers* at the moment is enjoying the serial strand, but that sort of thing - if the network didn't like it they'd cut it. But because *Stingers* is about to go into its 7th season it's got it's loyal audience, so you can be much more flexible with the rules once a show is established. You could never get away with that in the first or second year. We did a five parter at the end of the first series which rated very well and it didn't make the network nervous. But the foreign audience doesn't like it. Because they sometime split the series in half.

Paul Davies: And even show eps out of order.

Roger Simpson: Eps out of order. They drop eps that they don't like. For some markets there's too much violence or language that's inappropriate. So they just drop eps. And if they happen to be in the middle of a serial strand its a disaster. Distributors also don't like serials. The Network decided the serial element in *Snowy* was wrong but that was a wonderful era at 9. When David Leckie had just taken over and Bruce Gyngyll was there as well. A golden era. David Leckie was fantastic for Australian Drama. Very bold. Pretty unafraid of making big plays and riding with it to see if they came off. After *Snowy* we went into Channel 9 to the network meetings - this doesn't happen any more - to deal with the managers. Now it's all corporatised. But in those days you actually went to the Network meeting to pitch the second series of *Snowy* and they virtually said: we don't want to go with *Snowy* again but we like you guys and what you do, have you got anything else for us? And we virtually said on the spot. "What about Rebecca Gibney as a forensic psychiatrist?" They said, "fantastic we'll have six."

Paul Davies: Is that something you had in the bottom drawer?

Roger Simpson: It was something Roger and I sketched together out in the waiting area when we sensed that the mood of the Network meeting wasn't going to go in our direction. We decided we better have something up our sleeve. Rebecca was in *Snowy* and we thought there was potential to do something with her. So we had this idea. But there was nothing on paper. That was David Leckie. A very gutsy sort of call. Others were struggling to do one, or a maximum of three, telemovies and usually they would do one and see how it went. Whereas he just said 'Six' let's go for it.

Paul Davies: Simpson Le Measurier have always built their series around people like Rebecca Gibney, Marcus Graham (*Good Guys Bad Guys*) Magda Szbanski (*DogWoman*), Peter Phelps in *Stingers*...

Roger Simpson: The older and wilier you get you try to make every post a winner. When you're young and naive and idealistic and all you want to do is a series about the Vietnam War - even when the market didn't want it - it was the first series about the War- years before Kennedy Miller made *Vietnam*. We weren't even allowed to use the word 'Vietnam' in the title. Which is why we called it *Sword of Honour*. It was too raw and recent and Australian Television wasn't ready for it. So we had a love story set in South East Asia with the vague background of the war. And the peace movement - that was one thing, but the subject matter was unacceptable. We were driven in those days by the stories we wanted to tell, and to hell with boring detail like casting. Now its the other way round because we realise you develop a lot of things that never get made and you want to minimise the wastage and so my advice to young writers is think strategically from the beginning and by all means follow their hearts and passions but if you can make the package look more attractive by having some talent attached well, why not ?

Paul Davies: When you look at the slate of programmes that you've produced, police drama is very central to it. You have a background as a barrister and even your headquarters is the old police station in North Melbourne... what is it about crime on television that is so enduring as a genre?

Roger Simpson: It has the perfect dramatic form, the crime or problem or commission of the crime is the beginning, the middle is the investigation and the ending is the conclusion - guilty or not guilty. It just has the perfect dramatic form. We've been struggling at times, we've sort of given up now, but there was a time where we wanted to get free of the label of crime television. *Good Guys* was at one level, an attempt to get away from cop shows or legal shows but it was really a crime show. Just happened to be a crime fighting dry cleaner. As opposed to a policeman. I guess it's a bit in the blood. Some people write hospital drama, some people write family drama, our bag is crime. That's what we do. Over the years you pick up an awful lot about how the police force works. How the legal system works. You have all this knowledge and the tendency is to use it. Ever since I've been in television in Australia - 30 years now - they always say there's too many cop shows. As when Hector was making them in the early 70s. The critics still say it. But it's what people watch. The Americans keep making them and the English keep making them. *The Bill, CSI* etc.

Paul Davies: You mentioned the structural principle of the crime which coincides with the dramatic structure. Is there an element also of reassurance for the audience that there's somebody out there looking after them. That the good guys always win. Justice is seen to be done. We can all sleep a little safer in our beds tonight...

Roger Simpson: That's been the tradition and that's why in the past, shows about corrupt cops - except for short run things like *Blue Murder* (which is acceptable as four one hours). But in the past there's always been that conventional wisdom that the audience want reassurance. They don't like crooked cops. But in American now there's *The Sopranos*. And a new cop show called *The Shield* which has a bad cop in it. So there is a change happening but the bad cop needs a moral rationalisation.

Paul Davies: *Stingers* are playing with that idea at the moment, the Harris character appears to be corrupt for about six eps. But we find out in the end, of course, that he is on the side of the angels. But you play with this idea and lead the audience on. And from a writing point of view its a terrific dynamic because you can go against the convention and play on those irrational fears people all have - that if the guardians are corrupt then we're in trouble...

Roger Simpson: Yes.

Paul Davies: So there's a quirkiness, a playful larrikin aspect to a lot of Simpson Le Measurier shows. Going against the grain. Is that something that comes from you and Roger personally?

Roger Simpson: I think it's about embracing the Australian character because in our trips overseas we see that what makes our drama marketable is our difference. There was a period in the 80s when Australian drama was trying to be English or American drama. But going to the markets - what they like about us is the difference. That larrikin personality which is essentially Australian. Roger and I both have a cheeky outlook on life, so it suits our personalities to go that way, but it's smart too. And the quirkiness is sometimes a survival mechanism. It's a tough game and its always battling with survival. It's knife edge. It might look secure on the outside. But it's a precarious business as you know, Paul. It can blow up in your face and a show can be cancelled without warning. So part of the survival mechanism is to make the job as enjoyable as possible. Because you dare not worry about the future. So there's a larrikin attitude in our day to day working lives. Because if you were sensible you wouldn't be in the game at all. (laughs).

Paul Davies: I think it was Brecht who said if you're not having fun doing it, nobody's going to have fun watching it.

Roger Simpson: That's so true.

Paul Davies: There's also the question of logic in police drama. A lot of what the plot comes down to is - is this logical? The threading of the narrative is to do with logical coherence and rationality. A lot of the script editing is to do with fixing up the illogical in the story. Is this something that a barrister's eye gives you.

Roger Simpson: Are you talking dramatic logic or the authenticity of the police work?

Paul Davies: Both.

Roger Simpson: I had to unlearn a lot. The trouble with being a barrister is that it's all to do with precision. A legal document is meant to have no loopholes in it. I think when I became a writer I had to learn that precision doesn't make good drama. And the unexpected is probably what it's all about. But contradictory to that, it has to be within a logical world because you can't just sort of pull rabbits out of the hat unless you've thought it through and people can see that it's plausible. So there's these two dynamics in opposition to one another. One is authenticity, plausibility - the real world. But then drama hinges on surprise and the unexpected because you don't want people to work out where you're headed. Because if they can guess the ending they're going to be bored rigid.

Paul Davies: In a lot of *Halifax* too, there's that element of surprise, you could never accuse a *Halifax* script of being ahead of the audience. As much as the quirky larrikin element, there's that sense of the concealed mystery – which makes those stories stand out. In *Stingers* also to a certain extent.

Roger Simpson: The murder mystery was a lot of fun. There won't be any more *Halifax's* but we want to make more murder mysteries. It's as durable as the cop show. It's another form of TV drama that's been around since *Colombo, Murder She Wrote, McMillan and Wife* and the poms did it too. It's a pretty good form.

Paul Davies: When you're putting together a concept for a series are you looking for characters that are going to endure across 26, 52 hours or drama? Is it the setting, the characters, what grabs you first?

Roger Simpson: It's definitely character because if you don't get those right you're going to be very bored with writing them. But setting is part of character because the character dictates its setting. Sometimes you change the setting to suit the character- if that helps the character. There's a lawyer or a cop or a dry cleaner...but basically it (*Good Guys*) started off as a crime fighter on the wrong side of the law, a former cop. It's my favourite show.

Marcus Graham *Good Guys Bad Guys*

Paul Davies: So why don't we see more of *Good Guys*?

Roger Simpson: The network had a lot of trouble with it. It had a loyal audience that loved it. The Network felt it wasn't broad enough.

Paul Davies: Was it a young audience?

Roger Simpson: It was a young audience. Now - because the rules keep changing - now Channel 9 would be delighted to have a *Good Guys* because these days it's acceptable to target a particular demographic as opposed to a broad one. But in those days it was the broad demographic or nothing. So, because we were very niche focused in the audience, it never went beyond its second series. We had financial problems too. It was a very expensive show. Shot in seven and a half days with a lot of locations, a lot of stunts, it was pretty splashy television and it sold well in some markets. The French for example loved it. Apart from *Halifax* it was the only thing we ever sold to France. But it didn't finally get the sales to justify the big budget.

Paul Davies: Would you have done a slimed down version?

Roger Simpson: I don't think so. You can take *Stingers* into a studio, but *Good Guys* was much more action based, round the streets.

Paul Davies: I remember you saying once they were very hard to write, tricky...

Roger Simpson: Tricky, yes. Although we were getting team of writers towards the end who really latched on to it. But all new shows are hard to write.

Anne Phelan as "Mon" *Something In the Air* (2000-2002)

Roger Simpson: *Something In The Air* was hard to write at the beginning. And then it finds itself and the teams of writers all play their part as well. Somebody writes a script and you say, yeah, that's what we're trying to do. It's all teamwork. It doesn't matter how long you spend in preparation, everything has a shakedown period. Theory is one thing, you can write and rewrite scripts as much as you like but until you're actually making it; and until the directors and actors place their interpretation on the characters you've created... in the old days I tried to control those characters as I saw them. Once again, something you learn when you get a bit grey in the head- (laughs) you're better off letting the actors and directors play their role and add their dimension and not be so proprietorial about it.

Paul Davies: So you write the pilot scripts, you create the characters, you spend a certain amount of time in the story department and then you stand back?

Roger Simpson: You get the best results when you empower the people who are making the show. In the old days Roger and I were probably control freaks who wanted to be all over it. But all you're doing is undermining the people - everybody else who've got a huge contribution to make. With each series of *Stingers* I've done less and less. And with each series of anything there's a process of setting it up, then empowering the other people to play their part and that's when it's really exciting. Also my brief is to prepare for the next disaster (laughs). Errol Sullivan once said to me, there's only one thing certain in television: when a show is commissioned one day it will be axed. You don't know whether it will be the first series or the second series. But the axe is going to fall. So I've never forgotten that and I've always had two or three things. There were years where we didn't work and I had nothing ready. Now I'm working at three or four things at once. Because *Stingers* won't go on forever. *Halifax* went for Seven years. *Something In The Air* finished after two.

Paul Davies: Is there something more personal in the bottom drawer though - apart from the bread and butter stuff. Is there something where it didn't matter what the network wanted... or the demographic.

Roger Simpson: That will be known as the era of my bad novels. (laughs) The thing about TV is that it's a business. The good old days of the one-off play on the ABC are long gone. I've got a couple of plays I'm writing but you have a company to run and so you've always got to feed the monster.

Paul Davies: You've always had that loyal group of people around Simpson Le Measurier who have gone across a number of shows with you. Something reminiscent of the Crawford era. The engenderer of talent and the creators of teams of people...

Roger Simpson: Yeah. And I like that. I like the process. Roger and I always said to each other - and this is ridiculous after 30 years - it was a young man's game. Because you work long hours and it's relentless. Every day brings a new problem. And you get to a stage where you think the next generation can do this. Then I'll probably go to some shack in the bush and finish these plays. And they'll be personal and made by a regional theatre company...

Paul Davies: Plays rather than features or novels?

Roger Simpson: I think I'm a dramatist rather than a novelist. I'm more comfortable with dialogue and performance. Dramatic structure rather than the structure of a novel. I don't even know the rules for a novel. I don't mean I'd write bad plays. Just not mainstream. Not made for the big audience. We are unashamedly main stream television makers.

Paul Davies: Well there's no other form is there?

Roger Simpson: No. I think even the ABC unfortunately still wants to rate. So you can't. There's not much opportunity for a personal statement. I think there are other outlets for that. You are just wasting your time in television. A movie would be better. For a very personal statement.

Paul Davies: But there is that idea of the personal in the *Good Guys* style of television.

Roger Simpson: Oh yes.

Paul Davies: You couldn't confuse it with a *Blue Heelers* for example.

Roger Simpson: No. Absolutely not . When you're a writer. The personal. It's there in a *Stingers* script too.

Paul Davies: It's in the dialogue...

Roger Simpson: It's in the story, the guest characters. The situation. And there's tons of opportunity to say what you want to say about the big world around you.

Paul Davies: Then a script editor comes along and changes it all. (laughs)

Roger Simpson: Oh yeah. I like the editing process. Although I've never been an editor. Roger has been my editor. And he still is. So in the first instance, when you're writing a pilot. It's Roger who crits it. And he's very efficient. He only makes six or seven points. But they always go right to the heart. They tear it to bits. And then you've just got a pile of words sitting on the floor... He's not a line by line, he's a big picture editor. And he's extremely good at it. He always has been. I think his major talent as a producer is his nose for a script. And he's never wanted to write interestingly enough.

Paul Davies: So that's the perfect marriage isn't it. The writer and the editor.

Roger Simpson: I think so. The writer and producer. But it was a very lucky accident. We weren't close friends and we weren't... we never had plans... it was opportunistic rather than anything else. Le Measurier went across to New Zealand to be a producer, and we worked together a bit, writer-producer. Then he came back to Australia to do shows on a freelance basis. And then we tried this movie.(*Squizzy Taylor*).

Paul Davies: And you never looked back...

Roger Simpson: Well, it sounds good from this distance but the first ten years were pretty hairy.

Paul Davies: Were there moments when you thought this is not going to gel here?

Roger Simpson: No, we were realistic about it. You can take more risks when you're young and stupid too. Naivety is a wonderful thing. If we'd known what we know now we mightn't have stuck it through. But you always thought tomorrow was going to be a brand new day and the phone would ring and somebody would give us the money...

Paul Davies: So you've got to be optimistic.

Roger Simpson: Inane optimism.

Paul Davies: And then have fun doing it.

Roger Simpson: Yeah. Well we went to lunch a lot. It cheers you up. Your days start at 7 o'clock something. You can't write all day long. You can't produce all day long. It's a tough job. Then you're still doing meetings, correspondence, viewings and all that other stuff in the afternoon. But I've always marked the middle of the day with a bit of a reward (laughs).

Paul Davies: So do you have a typical working day? An ideal writing structure? Do you start at a certain time? Or wait for the muse...

Roger Simpson: I write every day. But I've got to be careful to have weekends. Because I'd go mad if I didn't. But there was a time when I didn't stop. A workaholic unfortunately - from a writing point of view. I'm happiest in my room tapping away and I'll do it at night, early in the morning. All day.

Paul Davies: There's deadlines too of course...

Roger Simpson: But a lot of the work I do its speculative so the deadlines are self imposed. It's just a bit manic and a bit compulsive. And the danger I've got is I've got to be careful to have a life.

Paul Davies: So it's not a matter of finding the switch so much as switching off?

Roger Simpson: My family protests. I make this Sydney-Melbourne thing work for me. Because at home with the family (in Sydney) I have a saner working life. Weekends and time with my children and catch up with friends. When I'm in Melbourne I just lock myself away and work day and night. And I love that too because its so self indulgent. Though it's not a way to keep friendships or marriages. Or relationships with children. So I confine my writing time in Melbourne and do it day and night. Unless I've got a script. Which I tend to write quickly.

Paul Davies: So a TV hour would take a week to write?

Roger Simpson: A week for the draft. Three to five days. And three to five for the treatment.

Paul Davies: The treatment is just as important. The Scene Breakdown stage?

Roger Simpson: More important. That' s when you establish your characters, the ending, the dramatic structure. All the rules. And so when I sit down to write the draft I know every scene. How long, who's going to be in them and I very very seldom stray from the scene breakdown. Whereas I know other writers hate them. It may be my legal training. I just like to know what it feels like before I leave home. And I hate rewriting, I absolutely loathe rewriting. And so I make damn sure I've solved the problems before I start.

Paul Davies: The structural problems...?

Roger Simpson: Yeah, and I think through the scenes in my head - as I'm doing the Scene Breakdown. So I sort of have an ability to dramatise it in my imagination. So by the time I start page one, I know what I'm writing. I can just about see it. I see the settings, I know the characters. The surprise is in the dialogue. Once characters start talking to one another I think shit, I didn't think they were going to say that!

Paul Davies: It surprises you. The way it comes out?

Roger Simpson: Because I write so fast, you release the characters, they're out of their cages and running like a dog race and you don't know which one is going to win necessarily and I change the dynamic within a scene, but I very seldom change a Scene Breakdown.

Paul Davies: And once you've committed that dialogue into the computer is that it?

Roger Simpson: Unless everybody's unhappy with it. Then I'm into rewrite hell, like every writer is. But I would try really hard to get people to lock off on the story. So I can say, but hang on, you liked that story, don't change the rules on me now. I know writers who loathe Scene Breakdowns and think it inhibits the creative process. For me I'm a structuralist from way back. In terms of creating TV series it's structure structure structure. It's characters, setting, what is the story engine...

Paul Davies: This was the Crawfords style wasn't it? I remember on the first day as a trainee script editor you were give a graph of the emotional structure they wanted for a Homicide episode. With a wriggly line showing the waves of emotional intensity from segment to segment.

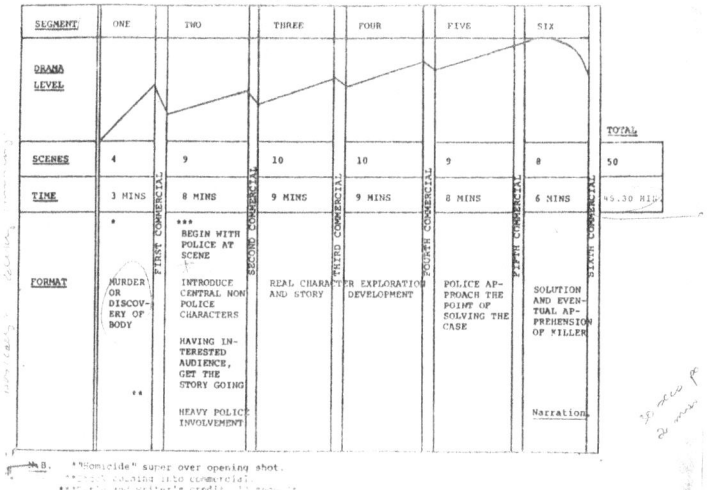

SEGMENT	ONE	TWO	THREE	FOUR	FIVE	SIX	
DRAMA LEVEL							
							TOTAL
SCENES	4	9	10	10	9	8	50
TIME	3 MINS	8 MINS	9 MINS	9 MINS	8 MINS	6 MINS	45.30 MINS
FORMAT	MURDER /OR DISCOV- ERY OF BODY	*** BEGIN WITH POLICE AT SCENE					
		INTRODUCE CENTRAL NON POLICE CHARACTERS	REAL CHARACTER AND STORY	CHARACTER EXPLORATION DEVELOPMENT	POLICE AP- PROACH THE POINT OF SOLVING THE CASE	SOLUTION AND EVEN- TUAL AP- PREHENSION OF KILLER	
		HAVING IN- TERESTED AUDIENCE, GET THE STORY GOING					
	**	HEAVY POLICE INVOLVEMENT				Narration	

(Vertical labels between columns: FIRST COMMERCIAL, SECOND COMMERCIAL, THIRD COMMERCIAL, FOURTH COMMERCIAL, FIFTH COMMERCIAL, SIXTH COMMERCIAL)

* "Homicide" super over opening shot.
** ... ... into commercial
*** ... ... writer's credit ...

The *Homicide* script template

Roger Simpson: It probably came from Dorothy (Crawford) who was a big influence. She and Ian Jones. But I love writing bibles. Even the bibles that never see the light of day. I love analysing what the story engine is going to be and putting your finger on it. And it's always a process of refining it down to this essential truth of what makes a series tick. You start with 50 pages, but the Writers' Bible is going to be a few paragraphs that nail it. You start with this big searching, outpouring on the computer which roams all over the place when you're looking for what makes the thing tick.

Paul Davies: The story engine.

Roger Simpson: And then you refine that 50 pages down to 30 then down to 10.

Paul Davies: So the first page has to nail it?

Roger Simpson: The first page, the one page after the 50 pages. It's the essence. It's the instant coffee but it comes from the plantation. It comes from the beans and drying it. Tons and tons of paper. I just pour every idea in my head into the computer. Then I print it out and stick it round the walls, then I circle bits and I'm trying to analyse and refine it down to the simple truth that makes that series unique.

Paul Davies: And that's the story engine?

Roger Simpson: That's the trick. In *Good Guys Bad Guys* it was a former cop from a criminal family. That's what it came down to. A crime-fighting dry-cleaner. It comes down to something as simple as that. It starts as a huge outpouring about god knows what - Tourette's syndrome - as all these occupations come pouring out and I tried him as a dry cleaner - which was a very late development. But you're looking for something that has got the right quirk.

So he actually hates dirt. It was a business he thought was going to be a bludge. It is a bludge because he hires someone to run it for him. But you don't start with that, you end up with that.

Paul Davies: So it's a journey.

Roger Simpson: A journey to that essence. From random jottings down to something which the writers, when they read them - my bibles aren't long - but they start off as great tomes. Also its the network too. Anyone who's going to be involved in it, directors, actors, everybody needs it in a nutshell.

Paul Davies: And as the series progresses, I remember at the end of *Something In The Air*, someone did a map of all the places and people and characters that were depicted in the show and it blows out again, there's this world you've created that has creeks and parks and mountains, other towns. And you think, this is a totally imaginary place, but it all comes from that one original story engine.

Roger Simpson: The tendency is for more and more information to be added as the series goes along. We refine that story engine on every series. Every series on *Stingers*, or *Halifax* or Something In The Air - we're trying to make that story engine more and more profound and perfect. It doesn't stop. Every series, its not quite that sentence - it's that sentence.

Paul Davies: So the engine will change?

Roger Simpson: You refine the bible all the time.

Paul Davies: *Stingers* has gone more internal, psychological, especially with the studio component to it now.

Roger Simpson: Because Roger and I have become less control freaks. *Stingers* has now become the personality of the people who work on it. As the story teams have changed the flavour of the show has changed. I guess your job as a producer is, if you can see them heading in the wrong direction, you stop it. But if it's going in the right direction... as long as its positive you go with that. But it's constantly refined and re-defined. It's a search for what makes the show tick.

Paul Davies: Can you talk about what the future holds for you now?

Roger Simpson: We're developing some telemovie possibilities.

Paul Davies: With a continuing character base?

Roger Simpson: Yes, generic telemovies- like *Halifax*. Last year we put a lot of energy into developing *Halifax* as a one hour series. A co-production with Linda La Plant. Unfortunately, that bit the dust when David Leckie left. Even though that series hasn't happened there's still a relationship with Linda La Plant so we're still keen on a co-produced crime show with her. Made in Australia with English elements. Co-conceived with Linda La Plant and me. We're also developing a new series for Channel 10. I've got three or four ideas fighting with each other in my head at the moment. And if they don't like the first one they'll get the second. But which ever one sells - that's the one I'll bond with. (laughs). But as Hemingway said: "A story told is never written" so I don't like to say too much until it's down on paper. Then I'll start showing it to people.

(Interview held at The Gypsy Café, Smith Street Collingwood. 26/9/2002)

The "Two Rogers" Le Mesurier and Simpson
"Roger and I have kept ourselves adaptable. Because the rules change."

BETWEEN FACT AND FICTION
(Speculating on the Documentary)
John Hughes
METRO # 136 (2003)

John Hughes trained as a news cameraman with the ABC before turning to the world of independent film making where his documentaries have been remarkable for their social and political content as well as their stylistic and visual experimentation. His credits include *Menace, Traps, All That Is Solid, One Way Street (Fragments For Walter Benjamin), River of Dreams,* and *After Mabo.* John also directed the feature *What I Have Written* based on a novel by John A Scott. He recently completed a four year term as Commissioning Editor For Documentary at the SBS.

Paul Davies: What is the documentary script? Is it a kind of contradiction in terms - given that documentaries sometimes are observational and only really exist in the film form first?

John Hughes: There is a tradition of the observational documentary but it's only one tradition. There's obviously an absolutely central tradition of the carefully, skillfully crafted documentary script from Joris Ivens and Grierson on... But the term 'script' is- in this context- a kind of generic term.

Paul Davies: Then is it more accurate to say that what you start with first is the 'documentary treatment'? Which sometimes of course bears very little relationship to what ends up on the screen. And may be just a process you go through to open up the money box at some funding body?

John Hughes: Well the treatment is an inherent part of the process. Because in a sense you're writing all the time.

Paul Davies: I remember Pat Laughren giving a paper at the Woodford Festival recently where he claimed that writing a documentary was really about writing a series of begging letters- first to the funding bodies to get the money to make it, then to the people you want to be in it...

John Hughes: That's stretching it a bit to consider the release form as part of the process of documentary writing. Or indeed signing cheques...(laughter).

Paul Davies: I think Pat was joking (sort of).

John Hughes: Different people work in different ways. And everybody produces different genres of writing at various stages of the production of the documentary. In the case of *Menace* (and I don't think this has fundamentally changed over the period I've been working), there are much finer distinctions between what is written and what the genre of the document is called. But recently, ABC and SBS for example, are saying they don't want well developed proposals. What they want is very short outlines of an idea and if they like that they'll tell you about how they think it should proceed from there. Both networks now have development money for documentary (something which has been very difficult to get in the past) and part of that is about a shift that seems to be taking place where the desire of television is occupying some of the territory that has previously been occupied by film filmmakers themselves in producing critical or observational intervention in the culture.

Paul Davies: So when you had your hat on as head of SBS documentary and people are coming along with their projects, what is it that you were looking for out of a particular proposal or treatment ?

John Hughes: If we can take a step back for a moment - let's say that an early document is a 'Proposal'- it's the description of the project - a few pages giving some background of the material that they want to work with and some information about what the narrative strategies are and what the treatment idea is - all of that is what you might call ' The Proposal'. If it's a reasonably thought-out Proposal it will have a treatment element as part of it. Which is not necessarily a synopsis of how the film will appear on the screen - that depends on the material it's dealing with. If it's dealing with an event that's unfolding in the present, then all the treatment can talk about is how it proposes to engage with those unfolding events.

Paul Davies: So something like *Year Of The Dogs* for example is going to be a film that follows a footy team through a season. But it's impossible to predict what will happen to the team... and therefore what the film will be about?

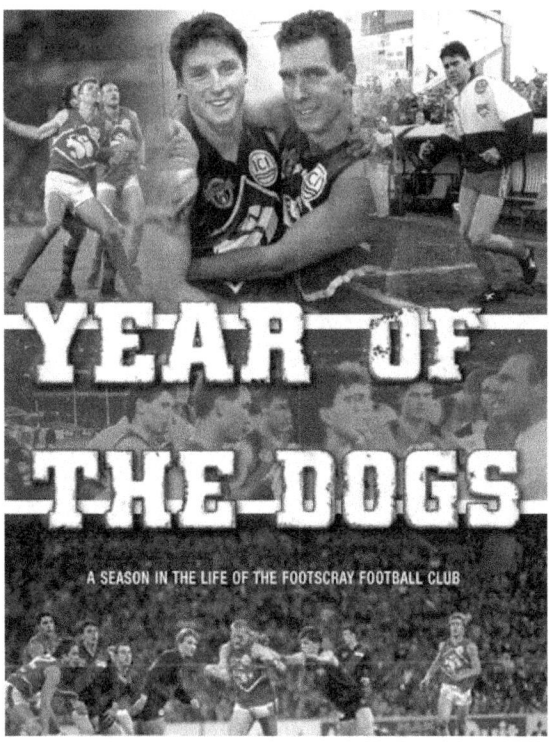

John Hughes: Yes, but the proposal is not going to be persuasive unless it's able to give you the information about what the context is and what's at stake for the team. Why it is likely to work dramatically.

Paul Davies: So you're looking for the dramatic potential in any given idea?

John Hughes: You're looking for engaging story elements certainly. But you're also looking for what is the pertinence of it. What does it have to say that is insightful more generally about the culture of the place. So - if they want to follow events during the course of a year in this particular football club then the question is why? And the available answers are "Well because they're really amusing people and they're great to watch." Okay, that's fine. That's one approach. Or its "Because the issues the football club are dealing with has much broader significance" . There are any number of possibilities.

Paul Davies: So in a film like *Traps* say, the subject is the Australian Labour Party and the way it is transformed by a key player like Bob Hawke, and the moments around which you build that story are things like the ALP conference in 1984 etc.

Prime Minister Bob Hawke shocked by an exploding light bulb
at the 1984 Labour Party Conference – *Traps* (1985)

John Hughes: Well *Traps* is a particular case because it's explicitly about trying to play with a mix of fiction and non-fiction. So it's a complicated example. But it's interesting to note that during the making of that film we were writing all the time, continually coming up with possible sequences to tell certain stories that were pertinent to what was going on around us in those months between 1983 and 1984. And that's one way that documentary script writing works: in that you will always be trying to find - in the material that you're dealing with - treatment ideas to get on screen what you think is important about the subject you've chosen to film.

Contemporary Arts Media - Artfilms

Caz Howard as "The Journalist" in *Traps*

TRAPS: In 1983 the Hawke Labour government came to power, establishing an administration of 'consensus' and was re-elected in '85. Carolyn Howard plays a fictional journalist, pursuing investigative political stories through actual tally rooms and newsrooms, meeting journalists, politicians and artists. Evoking histories of the Cold War and the events of November 11, 1975. *Traps* is a provocative blend of fact and fiction, news and disinformation, conspiracy theory and the packaging of politics.

Paul Davies: And then there's this thing you once called the 'Speculative Documentary'...?

John Hughes: That was about one way of thinking through this question, because one of the factors at that time (and it remains a problem) is that people use the term 'documentary' so generally that it becomes very difficult to talk sensibly about it because there are so many different approaches involved. So the term 'speculative documentary' was an invention of mine to try and specify a particular sub-category of the essay which had the character of saying: 'what we're dealing with here is a work of the imagination'.

Paul Davies: So we're entering a genre here that is neither fictional nor documentary. But as you say, more like an essay or speculation on certain ideas...

John Hughes: Which doesn't make it other-than-documentary. It just means that the term 'documentary' has to be recognized as a word that encompasses a wide range of traditions. So you can look at a particular film and find the fine threads of a variety of traditions that make their way into it.

Paul Davies: Is it more appropriate therefore to think of all films as basically telling some kind of story, whether it's preconceived and acted out (the narrative drama) or whether it's captured and reassembled in different ways in the editing suite (the documentary). And in both cases what we're really hoping for is some kind of engagement with an audience in order to bring about change - or at best distraction...

John Hughes: I think a lot of my stuff has got an agit prop dimension. But there are other agendas too.

Paul Davies: So what prompted you to undertake a project like *What I Have Written* ? Was the narrative feature a step you'd always wanted to take?

John Hughes: Not really, it was simply getting hold of a manuscript of John Scott's novel as a work in progress and finding it very engaging and feeling that it was dealing with important material and then thinking that the only way to do this was as a narrative drama .

Jacek Koman as Jeremy Fliszer in *What I Have Written* (1996)

Paul Davies: And yet the style of the film (for want of a better word) the use of stills - gives it a kind of documentary feel. The frozen images in that film are like captured moments of reality. It also shares with your other work a kind of excitement about the image, a kind of playfulness with form and editing.

John Hughes: When the Philippine bishop, Cardinal Sin, was asked how, as a committed Christian, he could justify the relationship between his church and the dictator Ferdinand Marcos he said it was a kind of 'critical collaboration'. So I guess the 'playfulness' you talk about there in the films for me is a 'critical collaboration' with orthodox ways of speaking. And that comes up in films like *Traps* and *All That Is Solid* – both films are engaged in a critical collaboration with orthodoxy. And part of that is an exploration of the poetic dimension of image and story. In relation to *What I Have Written* you're right, the themes that are central to that narrative are exactly concerned with the telling of stories and their relationship to actuality. And the troublesome status of that relationship.

Paul Davies: It's also a film about a specific 'document'- a piece of writing that has a disputed authorship.

John Hughes: Yes. That's one of the things I responded to in the book that Scott was writing. They were parallel concerns to what I had been doing in all those previous films.

Paul Davies: So what role if any, is there for the dramatic reconstruction in the documentary? Does it depend on the project- is it a matter of what's appropriate or is it just part of the tool box of the film maker? Because I suppose it's also about resources...

John Hughes: Well there's dramatic reconstruction and there's dramatic reconstruction.

Paul Davies: For example, in *One Way Street* - it took the form of a kind of 'speculative reconstruction' perhaps? I'm thinking of the scenes there between Walter Benjamin and Asja Lakis - which are not even pretending to be real in a sense, but are a kind of 'embellished drama'.

Nick Lathouris as Walter Benjamin in *One Way Street* (1992)

John Hughes: We used to call it 'stylized reconstruction'. But the word 'reconstruction' becomes a bit redundant in that sense. And 'dramatic reconstruction' in documentary at this stage doesn't have a real lot of use for me. It's not the kind of, taken for granted form, that it once was - you know the 'dramatic documentary' – the drama which sought to tell a true story as accurately as it could using actors, dialogue, sets and costumes - that's much less common now. But the tradition lives on and you see it in works like *The Realm of the Hackers* (written and produced by Kevin Anderson, produced by John Moore) where what you have on the screen are illustrations of events the protagonists in the film describe.

In the Realm of the Hackers (2003)

There's a certain kind of realist naturalism that occurs in that tradition. At some point there was a strong critique among documentarists of that realist naturalism as a mode in documentary on the grounds that it made claims about its legitimacy which were very hard to sustain.

Paul Davies: So it became a suspect methodology?

John Hughes: Yes. And there are a couple of ways that criticism emerged- partly through people writing about it. And also through the development of strategies in certain films that directly attack it. And the way to directly attack it seemed to me to be to make those moments of illustration explicitly fictional and not seek to have them perform as realist naturalism. But have them perform as a kind of poetic moment. And once you decide on that strategy it's about finding the aesthetic means to achieve it.

Paul Davies: Which is the quality of those scenes in *One Way Street* that are quite deliberately unrealistic. Staged almost.

Paul Davies, John Hughes on the set of *One Way Street* (1992)

John Hughes: In that case and in other cases, the strategies used have readable significance which is not explained but have to be teased out of it by the spectator. They can either read it or not. But the poetic, fragmented images in *One Way Street* are much more set pieces. Whereas, I think of things like *50 Years Of Silence* that Carole Sklan wrote and Ned Lander directed, which sought to produce emotive and evocative historical moments in the life of the protagonist (events from the 1940s). In that film there were a series of highly stylized poetic images that the writer designed that allow you to connect with the story in an emotional way without implicitly making the claim that this is what it was really like - or what really happened. So that becomes a convention and orthodoxy in itself.

Paul Davies: So the speculation about what happens needs to be transparent speculation?

John Hughes: It's not as though people who are watching realist drama don't know they're watching something that has been written and manufactured for that purpose.

Paul Davies: There's a suspension of disbelief though that goes on in narrative drama to the extent that a lot of the audience apparently think the actors make up the words themselves. (laughs)

John Hughes: In the documentary, of course they do. And in *Traps* so did the actors - I'm thinking of John Flaus's priest for example. But that was part of the playfulness of that film.

Ericka Addis, Paul Davies, James Grant
on location in Canberra for *Traps* (1985)

Paul Davies: So was Walter Benjamin a major influence on your work - Art in the Age of Mechanical Reproduction, the fragmentary nature of existence and creativity? Searching for the revelation...

John Hughes: Yes, I'm interested in Benjamin and I'm still discovering things. Working my way through. It's not so much the Artwork essay. It changes at different points. Trying to understand his work. I keep going back to it. One of the reasons it's so rich is because in some ways it's very complex and has so many layers.

Paul Davies: And lots of readings.

John Hughes: I think so. But part of the beauty of it is that you can use it- both the methods Benjamin employs to write and the material that he's dealing with, and the creative ideas that he develops. You can apply them critically.

Paul Davies: A recent project you were working on was *Australian Nations.*

John Hughes: Yes, I spent most of last year working with Rachel Perkins and a number of writers, basically doing research for a series of seven or eight one hours on an Aboriginal history of Australia. I'm now working on a project which is inspired by a recent book of Dennis Atlman's. And I'm interested in something on the Australian film industry. But that's at an early stage.

Paul Davies: And the title of your company – "Early Works"- Does that imply the best is yet to come?

John Hughes: Of course. (laughs)

(Interview at *Lo Spuntino* Cafe, Acland Street, St. Kilda 22/2/03)

CRIME, POLITICS AND THE GIRL

An Invisible Logical connection
Shane Maloney
METRO #142 (2004)

Of the five "Murray Whelan" novels written by Shane Maloney, two have just been produced as telemovies for the Seven Network. *Stiff* was adapted and directed by John Clark and the second, *The Brush Off* (also screen written by Clark) was directed by Sam Neill. Both episodes star David Wenham in the Murray Whelan role with Mick Malloy as his hapless boss, Angelo Agnelli – minister for various portfolios in various State Labour governments. A cast of real Labour luminaries make cameo appearances as themselves including: Barry Jones, John Button, Joan Kirner (former Victorian Premier), and current serving Premier, Steve Bracks. Other titles in the Murray Whelan series of novels include *Nice Try, The Big Ask,* and *Something Fishy.*

Paul Davies: Murray Whelan works for the Labour Party…

Shane Maloney: He's a Labour party functionary. It depicts someone in their world with a degree of affection. What's interesting about the Labour Party is its self mythologizing. It also sceptically examines its own self mythologizing. In a way that the Liberal party just doesn't. Which makes it both attractive and tragic at the same time. And allows it to kind of dangle this hope. It used to be said that the difference between the Liberals and Labour is about half an inch, but it's that half inch in which we manage to live. I worked for local government in Brunswick where I had been a community arts officer. And then for Melbourne City council as a cultural bureaucrat. I could do things. I could organize events, write letters from which all meaning had been bled. I was clearly someone suited to work in the corporate sector or in government. But I wasn't a team player. So when Melbourne failed to secure the Olympic bid I realized after 18 months on that particular job I had been exposed to organized crime in a sense. I had my subject matter.

Paul Davies: So you wrote a book about the Olympics?

Shane Maloney: Yes. And I also realized that it would be impossible to tell that story.

Paul Davies: Because of defamation issues?

Shane Maloney: Yes. Some of the (Olympic) bids around the world, their essential purpose was to advance people's careers and for that to happen entire cities had been persuaded to spend forty-sixty million dollars on an entirely quixotic project.

Paul Davies: Was this the basis for (the third Murray Whelan novel) *Nice Try* ?

Shane Maloney: *Nice Try* used part of it after the story broke. But what happened was, I wrote an airport novel. Big cover, embossed type, 800 pages, two athletes compete in the arena at the Olympic games and twenty/thirty years later are competing to be president of the IOC. And in the meantime the sweeping epic of the Olympics from a sort of amateur event to a global brand name is told as well. So I sat down and wrote a 150,000 word novel. After a while I realized there were severe problems with it. One of them was that the characters were wooden. Like a Tom Clancy novel – the kind of novel I didn't read myself. Plot driven. One dimensional characters. Dialogue that existed only to advance the story, provide information. Nobody was even really alive in it. And while there are people who can write those kinds of novels very successfully I realized I wasn't one of them. There were two lessons. One, that I could write big slabs of descriptive prose. The other thing was that I wasn't in good faith with my material. And therefore it didn't have any life. The animating spark wasn't there.

Paul Davies: It must've been hard though, having invested so much time, to finally to ditch the project...

Shane Maloney: I was also writing a monthly humour column for *Arena* magazine. So I was the funny page in the Marxist journal. And people liked that. The take, the humour. It occurred to me that what I should do was find a story which could be a vehicle for my social observations. And that it should be something I knew about. Not researched. But something I was intimately connected with. So that it would be a smaller novel. Write smaller, write local, something that used my voice. And all that came together in the creation of Murray.

Paul Davies: So why the crime genre?

Under Arrest - Shane Maloney

Shane Maloney: Because it's got a plot. A story. My recurring joke is that I have a character who must be both a hero and a member of the Labour Party. So I thought I would write that out. I want someone who, when he does save the day, does so entirely by accident. He's filled with good intentions. Doesn't wear his heart on his sleeve. People describe him as cynical. But he is appropriately sceptical. In fact he's far too sceptical to be a member of the Labour Party.

Paul Davies: One of the great shadings of Murray is the single dad thing. It gives him a certain humanity inside a world of politics that is essentially indifferent to the personal side. I guess the question is: why does a man with such good intentions remain inside an obviously corrupt system?

Shane Maloney: He describes it as being a member of a family, this large, dysfunctional family. I see Murray as the team player who is at the same time the outsider. It's a two party world. And he knows which party he's with. He does ruminate on the Tories "nosing the gates of power open with the bumper bars of their Rolls Royces". On the other hand he's also existentially dismayed at the crowd which, of necessity, he's stuck with. So he doesn't think much of the individuals that comprise his team; but it is the only team he could ever see himself playing for. The amount of corruption per se that he meets is of course very slight compared with the very genuine, very real corruption that he would encounter in that world.

Paul Davies In *The Brush Off*, when Murray gets the money at the end, he gives it back to Agnelli.

Arts Minister Angelo Agnelli (Mick Malloy) and Murray Whelan
(David Wenham) *The Brush Off* (2004)

Shane Maloney: He does it because the minister has blown the re-election funds on a bad investment. That's the 'McGuffin' in this story. *The Brush Off* begins when Murray goes back to the office and finds there's been a cabinet reshuffle and he overhears a conversation and he realizes his boss is doing something which he shouldn't do for this own sake and the party's sake. So when an opportunity arises to fix that, Murray does. He walks away having done his job. And that's the extent of his professional ethics.

Paul Davies: He does it to keep his job too. Which is constantly under threat. But we get the feeling there's something more to it all than just having an income.

Shane Maloney: It's his personal code. That's why, as Murray advances through the ranks, he follows the standard career path of a Labour party apparatchik- pretty much exactly: electorate officer, ministerial advisor, member of parliament and in due course he'll be a minister and his old minister will be his advisor. (Laughs.)

Murray Whelan (David Wenham) in a spot of bother

Paul Davies A lot of the narrative hinges on Murray getting himself into trouble. Getting into a hole literally - stuck in the basement (*The Brush Off*) - or in *Something Fishy* he's stuck on a buoy out in the Great Southern Ocean. It's all about him getting into difficulty, digging himself in deeper, then clawing his way back and not only solving the crime, but also he gets the girl. Or we're left at the end with the URST (UnResolved Sexual Tension) established and maybe he gets the girl, or maybe he doesn't, we're not sure...

Shane Maloney: He doesn't get the girl in *Stiff* because he's not completely free to get the girl - yet. Because his wife has gone off to pursue her career and she's doing better than he is. And he cops all of that. He doesn't have a problem with the fact that his wife is more successful. It's not a challenge to his manhood. It's just - she was a bitch. In a way. And she will eventually go off and revert to type. She's a girl from the eastern suburbs and she's had a bit of a dalliance with fashionable political and feminist issues and that's when he connected with her. We don't know why they broke up. Only that they have and she's just too full-on for him. So he doesn't get the girl. Then he does get the girl. By the third book the girl's gone and there's another girl.

Paul Davies: But there's always a girl. And there's always his son.

Shane Maloney: I'm having trouble with the sixth book because they're constructed from his personal life up. I start from his personal life and it's: how can things come into his life that set the story in motion? If you've got a cop or private eye - well, they go to the office in the morning and there's a dead body sitting on the desk and there's a note from the boss saying: 'Dead body, solve crime'. Whereas Murray has no reason to encounter a dead body, or a crime. If he does he'd call the police like everyone else.

Paul Davies Unless he's suddenly working for the Minister of Police.

Shane Maloney: But they're out of power.

Paul Davies: But it's fiction. You can make it up. You can bring them back.

Shane Maloney: No I can't. This is the problem with this character. I think he has been successful. And for a book (*Stiff*) to be in print for 10 years... The books that won the Premier's Literary Awards that year - they're no longer in print. It's like having the novel published in the first place. It's of that order.

Paul Davies: And there's another order of success which is getting the books made into telemovies. How did that come about?

Shane Maloney: There'd always been an interest from the very first book from film-makers. *Stiff* was optioned, then *The Brush Off* was optioned. In fact I was commissioned to write the screenplay by Andrew Knight.

Paul Davies: Which you did?

Shane Maloney: Which I did. But Andrew had moved on to *Siam Sunset* and *Seachange* was looming on the horizon...

Paul Davies: So that script wasn't used by John Clark?

Shane Maloney: No. I co-wrote that with someone and I accepted a lot of the assumptions. I was just told: 'well obviously he had to get the girl...'

Paul Davies: So they were changing the book?

Shane Maloney: Yeah the book was changed. And that was just the first draft. But by then it was clear that they weren't going to proceed (Artists Services). Initially when there was film interest, I of course got excited; and then I learnt after about three or four of these approaches and after I'd sold the rights, I just learnt not to be too excited. Show me the money, that was it. Because it was a world I knew nothing about. I had no control over it. Being a novelist is the ultimate mono-maniacal activity. You can't delegate even if you wanted to. You have complete control over your own material. So I'd go off and write another book and get some progress report (on the film option) and it would fall over or... what usually happens is that people just stop. They don't ring you up. Then after six months you ring them up and they don't return your call.

Paul Davies: Did you have an agent?

Shane Maloney: I had Rick Raftos for a while, but I'd already done the deal when I went to them and I think what I learnt from them was that it would be good if I was in Sydney - went to cocktail parties and things like that. There are also very practical rights as to what I'm selling. Am I selling the storyline? Am I selling the character? If so, how many storylines? Because any contract is going to use the word 'sequel' and this shocking neologism, 'prequel'- so the investors want to tie up everything that comes within a million miles of the original property. The T shirt rights, the golf shoe rights. All have to be negotiated and dealt with. So if I'm selling you the *Brush Off*, is the prequel rights to that, *Stiff* ? If those stories are already written, is it a case of buy one get two free ? No thanks.

Paul Davies: Nevertheless an agreement was made for *Stiff* and *The Brush Off* for the Seven Network...

Shane Maloney: The computer in 2001 had to be used to write the contract. It involved most of the computing capacity on Earth. (laughs). The fact that we were in furious agreement and wanted a contract that would express this did not in any way deter the lawyers from going at each other like pit bulls. I have a theory that film funding agencies artificially suppresses the price the novelist can expect to get for their work and often that's why we're seeing very poorly developed films on the screen.

Paul Davies: So how exactly did the translation from page to screen happen?

Shane Maloney: People always say the books are very filmic. They're not really because they're a first person narrative. So there are bits that might be vivid but that's because I've managed to persuade them to project the right images into their minds. It's quite odd really. It's part of the artifice of a novel to make a reader feel like he's watching a movie. And that way, all of the expense of the camera work, the lighting, and costuming and casting is put onto the reader. The consumer pays for the movie. Apart from some conversations with John (Clark) in the initial stages of the script and John ringing me up at three and four drafts along the way and asking me what I meant by this in the book or if this happened where was he (Murray), or why did he do this?... And I had to wrack my mind because there must've been some logical reason why it was in there. Because both of the books happen over a very precise period of time. Because if you look at my manuscripts you will find that I've got the time down the side. Virtually sentence by sentence. When he's stuck in *The Brush Off* he appears to be locked in a building in the pre-mobile phone era because I needed him out of action for three hours for the story to work. So I had to lock him somewhere. Once I had him down there and door is slammed I wrote a little scene and it became a whole other thing.

Murray locked in a lift with male ballet dancers
The Brush Off (2004)

Shane Maloney: Whereas with *Stiff* there are a number of scams happening that are not connected with each other at all.

Paul Davies: Which is potentially confusing.

Shane Maloney: Oh yeah, what I discovered was that while in the novel, particularly a crime novel, you need a certain amount of plot just to hold the structure up. In film, no matter how complicated the plot appears to be, it has to be fairly simple. And less is more and you create tension in all sorts of ways. There's much less information you can convey. I was interested (in the *Brush Off)* in the idea that a curator could approach a major art collector and say, "look I'm in a position to raise some serious doubts about the provenance or the authenticity or the value of your art collection and so if you don't pay me I can create financial difficulties for you".

Paul Davies: Which is easy to say but fraud always seems difficult to capture on film because essentially it's about dodgy paperwork.

Shane Maloney: It's about paper work. It's about perception. It's about a nod and a wink. And even in the book that conversation was never made explicit. So John (Clark) would ring me up and we'd talk about these things. And I clearly had a lot of confidence in John's ability to deal with the character, the nature of that world, the fact that it's all pretty chaotic. Then David Wenham's name came up as an attachment for it… he was involved very early in the piece which meant that he must have read the books. So that was nice. You see the character is never described in the book. Physically never. For the obvious reason that the reader can inhabit the character. Soon as you give the character a single physical characteristic you immediately exclude the reader from thinking they are inside that person's head, skin, whatever…

Paul Davies: Whereas it's almost the first thing a screen writer does. It sometimes starts with the casting.

Shane Maloney: Yes. So people would come to me and say who is your idea of Murray Whelan? And I'd say, well Gerard Depardieu. (laughs) That master of disguise…

Paul Davies: What, so he wasn't available? (smiling)

Shane Maloney: I didn't really think about it. So, when David Wenham's name came up I thought: 'well, why not? That's pretty good'… and then Sam (Neil) was brought on as a director - any reservations you have about your work being treated by other people sort of disappears at that point. You might not be 100% delirious about everything they've done with it but I can't imagine anyone else that I could repose that much confidence in.

Paul Davies: There's still three novels to go (*Nice Try, The Big Ask, Something Fishy*). Will we see them as telemovies?

Shane Maloney: They've got an option on another two - if Channel 7 are happy. And that means if it gets an audience and that depends on when they put it on… if it works for them they will commission the other two. Another book has been published since. The notion is that I'm running ahead throwing books over my shoulder. And they're coming up behind and turning them into two telemovies a year.

Paul Davies: Would it be like a *Halifax*- type operation? With a team of writers dreaming up Murray Whelan plots?

Shane Maloney: That's one way it could go. It does seem unthinkable to a novelist that you could delegate. Obviously it's got attractions. After six novels that are in the first person voice you begin to repeat yourself. I'm very concerned that characters begin to say the same things over and over again. The same expressions. Same Les Pattersonisms. You mine the Australian vernacular as many times as possible - like 'her nipples were as hard as Chinese algebra' - they become harder to find.

Paul Davies: But if you've got the character and you've got the same basic situation... Television does it all the time, things are given and writers have to invent.

Shane Maloney: That's why it's attractive. There are two reasons people become writers: indolence and vanity. The pay off is in the vanity. So you have to overcome your natural indolence in order to write something that results in people saying 'that was good...' You could (delegate and) swing the indolence side in. But if you did that why would you keep writing novels? I can think of plenty of Murray Whelan stories.

Paul Davies: All you need is a storyline.

Shane Maloney: There are three components to a Murray Whelan story. There is the crime plot. The political plot. And the girl/kid thing. Now the kid is seventeen.

Paul Davies: So he'd leaving home in about ten, fifteen years?

Shane Maloney: Yeah, well he's doing VCE this year. So it's: what subjects is he doing? He's going to Wesley, catching the bus...

Paul Davies: Does the single father thing then tend to trail off a bit?

Shane Maloney: That's why logically there are only two more books. There's one now where Red is seventeen - fifteen in the last one. He'll either turn out very organized - the opposite to his father. Go off and do an MBA or Science. Or he's going to present some crisis to Murray by dropping out and nicking off. But I don't know if I can keep doing that...

Paul Davies: Red seems to be the more sensible half of the team. Down to earth, grounded.

Shane Maloney: And quite capable of looking after himself. Although he did go off with that dingbat in the bushes at Lorne. A girl he was chasing (Jodie Prentice in *Something Fishy*).

Paul Davies: While his father was drowning off the beach.

Shane Maloney: It was a valuable learning experience for him. The last (Murray Whelan) novel will take place on Crete where Murray goes for a parliamentary delegation to lay a wreath for the fiftieth anniversary of the Battle of Crete and there's some tie in with the Greeks in Thornbury, and I know how I'm going to get Murray off the hook of the Labour party - he will do a Dmitry Dolos – the shadow minister for planning during the Kennett years who made no bones about the fact that he wasn't interested in being in politics and not in power. He kept nicking off to Greece. I want to do that with Murray - where he's got to save one of his father's old mates from the war or something, and at the same time there's an interesting Greek woman putting the moves on him, and Red's there doing a masters in Archaeology. I don't know the exact setup. But Murray will be de-selected, Labour will be back in power, he will have been successfully shafted by someone close to him at a time when he thinks, "ah fuck it who cares" and he'll have 8 years of super- two terms of super.

Paul Davies: Comfortable enough for the Mediterranean lifestyle.

Shane Maloney: He'll have sun. Backpacking around Europe. He's got the babe.

Paul Davies: Running a taverna on some Island. Going back to the pub. Back to his roots.

Shane Maloney: Exactly, he'll do what his father did. Run a pub. And it'll be the male equivalent dream of *My Life In Tuscany*.

Paul Davies: So that's it. Exit Murray?...

Shane Maloney: As far as the books go. It gets harder and harder. I have to be in good faith with him (Murray). I can't just get him to do things because I want to. No matter how creaky and outlandish these plots appear to be there should always, somehow, be an invisible, logical connection between one sentence and the next. It's that incremental thing about politics as well. It's – if you look at way things move over time you can discern a logical thread running through it all. But on a day to day basis…it never quite appears like that.

"There are two reasons people become writers:
indolence and vanity. The pay off is in the vanity."

(Interview held at Shane Maloney's place, East Brunswick 25/5/2004)

MY LIFE IN SOAP
Joe Deegan
METRO #146/147 (2005)

> Joe Deegan, lover, body surfer and scriptwriter, originally appeared in the novel, *33 Postcards From Heaven,* by Paul Davies (Gondwana Press, 2004), and still 'scribbles for a living' from his beach shack on the fabled Rainbow Coast of Northern New South Wales - which he shares with his occasional partner Barbara Solomon. Joe (sans agent) is currently under-employed and available for contract work on any local series or serial. The following is an extract from his diary over a couple of months some years ago... the images are taken from *33 Postcards From Heaven – Gateway To the Rainbow Coast* (Gondwana Press 2005)

22nd September EXT. CASA DEL FIBRO (MY BACK DECK)
CAST: ME

Casa del Fibro

I'm lying in the hammock, contemplating a second body surf to overcome some really depressing headlines:

"Aussie Dramas Take Local Anaesthetic!"

"Where Are The Viewers?"

"The Big Turnoff"

" 'Siggy' to the Rescue - Can She Save Our Industry, <u>Again</u>!?"

...the tabloids shriek.

And it hurts, because I have a confession to make. In the last three decades I've killed nineteen people - half a dozen serially, some by accident, others involving poison or guns. I've been married twenty times, suffered or celebrated eleven divorces (often from the same woman); and along the way, fathered thirty eight children (that I know about). I've burgled lonely milkbars or held up defenseless, but profiteering, service stations in order to fund an addiction to illicit drugs. I've settled feuds between families, cured rural animals of numberless ailments, and have betrayed, or at best, cruelly mislead most of my significant others. I've also participated in one ménage à trois, and deux ménage à quatres.

Yes, I am for my sins, forgive me dear diary, an Australian teledramatist. And therefore one of those partly responsible for the miserable crop of headlines above.

This is how I know that "Siggy" (aka Sigrid Thornton) cannot save our industry. Nor can any of her colleagues: the many talented local actors who have given us such wonderful renditions of who we are, and how we speak and love and hate each other over so many years of hits and misses on all the networks.

They can't do it because actors acting alone (without the aid of writers) are not a pretty sight. You only have to look at the abysmal failure of most 'improvised' film, theatre and television to realise this. The meaningless, circulatory exchanges of dialogue (that seem to run longer than an American Series' opening credits), all such scenes leave audiences catatonic with boredom. (Did some one say "*Wildside*"?)

Elsewhere, in the so called example of "Reality" (sic) television, untrained twenty-somethings are plunged into a synthetic prison where they engage in acutely embarrassing behaviour while trying to pretend that their every waking and sleeping moment isn't being closely monitored by millions of people. Could anything be less 'real'?

Clearly actors <u>need</u> words - the words writers give them to say inside the carefully nuanced plots we have constructed for their 'characters' to inhabit. Dentists put instruments, a writer puts <u>words</u> in other people's mouths. That's their job. It's what teledramatists do. Why people like me are so vital and necessary. When will anybody with the power to do something about it finally comprehend this fundamental fact!? Writers are experts in the frailty and vanity of human behaviour. We only need to look at ourselves for the research.

Unfortunately, for Australian producers, there is no hollywood-ised, bankable star-system in place that will guarantee bums on lounge suites in both western Sydney and eastern Melbourne. Attempting to capture these two markets simultaneously is the black hole into which most local dramas fall. If a show rates well in only one city it is doomed to being swiftly bumped to some demeaning, late-night timeslot. Where it quickly withers and dies. It takes a huge amount of cunning and misrepresentation to appeal to two such dissimilar audience catchments. One shamelessly material and shallow, the other intellectually snobbish and inward looking.

So "Siggy" can't save us, nor can any other actor or producer or director...

A cheeky currawong comes up and sits on my work table, leaving its calling card on the scene breakdown for the next episode of *On Golden Sands* - the soapie I currently soil for my living on. It seems a fitting comment. One critic was kind enough to call *OGS* "an appalling joke. So bad it isn't even laughable". I think of the arrogance of birds and all the heart and soul I have poured into this show. Only to see my sparkling dialogue and witty choreography blanded out by the team of young script editors coming up behind me. I think of the Roman Eagle, and how it was copied and ripped off by the Nazis.

23rd Sept. EXT. MY BACK DECK

CAST: ME (again, unfortunately)

Pandanaceae Gloriosa

Point Paradise

Wind a light nor' easterly picking up a perfectly curling break off Point Paradise. Will have first body surf after wake-up skinny cap.

Yet my depression congeals. The bad headlines are working up to a media frenzy. All the dreaded opinion writers have now picked up on an easy story. A free bash at the tall poppies:

"Local Series Flop!"
"Another Slump In Ratings!"
"Surviving A Week Of Oz On The Box"
"ABC Cuts Production Slate For Fourth Year"

The one thing Australians love more than success is outright failure. You know your career's in trouble when words like 'flop', 'slump', 'surviving' or 'cuts' start appearing in the opinion writers' pretty limited vocabulary.

The problem is so bad, the elision of the writer so complete, that most viewers do now actually think the actors make up the words themselves! How self-effacing and low status can my profession get? Anyone who knows anything about acting or writing quickly realises that most soapie stars are barely capable of forging their own Logie nominations - let alone write down or hold in their limited intellects anything so sensitive and delicate as an actual dramatic idea...

Can't the hack journos get it through their thick heads!? What's wrong with local teledrama is that the writer has virtually disappeared from the process!

Not just from the pages of the trade magazines (where we've hardly ever been conspicuous), but quite literally from the interminable opening credit sequence at the head of each episode (now sometimes running halfway into the programme!). I know, because I carefully scrutinize the names, wondering how people with such limited talent could get on the active writers' list of shows that didn't even respond to my CV.

I watch enviously as the Production Designer, Casting Agency, Best Boy and Third AD all get a guernsey and I wait in vain to see who wrote the obvious shambles that's about to follow (since no one is prepared to put their name to the thing in the box once marked 'author').

Call me an unreconstructed hippy romantic idealist, but I firmly believe that the soul of any dramatically realised enterprise is intimately connected to the soul of the person who dreamed up the thing in the first place. And in many cases now, that original, unique identity is being split in half.

The process of 'storylining' (plot wrangling) has been systemically divorced from the process of dialogue writing. With the predictable end result that nothing terribly eccentric, dangerous, visionary, or different can filter through the many layers of intellectual, egotistical and proprietorial gatekeeping that scars and damages any TV script on its painful journey towards final shooting draft (with pink amendments). Nobody is bold or adventurous or just plain free enough to be crazy any more.

I drop the offending and offensive newspapers into the compost bin, ignite a mid-morning "pick-me-up" – sourced from an excellent grower near Nimbin, and allow my gaze to wander out across Casa Del Fibro's backyard - my own little handkerchief of Paradise - flashing on the fact that the whole idea of a garden is to produce flowers. Insight still on track. Thank Gaia.

Besides, if drugs in sport are no-no, drugs in writing are a virtual prerequisite.

24th Sept.　　　INT.　　　MY OFFICE/GARAGE
CAST: ME (yes, still me!)

Author at work

Dear Diary, this morning's workload (two scenes) dashed off in under twenty minutes. New record. Leaves afternoon free for leisurely stroll to Point Paradise.

Reduced again to mere dialoguing! We used to call ourselves 'screenwriters'! What a joke. How often have I stared, incredulous, at the awful tripe one of my scripts gets reduced to on air. Watching alone, at home, like the few hundred other tragic losers capable of staying up until *On Golden Sands'* post-midnight timeslot... barely alive in front of the box, waiting with zombie-like concentration for the next batch of ads for softer beds, faster food, or more powerful stimulants - all the rubbish that people awake this time of night so obviously need.

Can't they see? Don't the networks get it!! It's only shows that have been the outcome of a single writer, or small-scale writing partnership, that put the runs on the board: *Mother And Son, Sea Change, Blue Murder, The Scales Of Justice, Kath & Kim, Changi, Love My Way* and *The Secret Life Of Us.* It's only when the <u>writer</u> is in charge that it ever really works.

Why do the network gatekeepers, in their sheltered workshops, have to learn the same lesson over and over again? You can make a bad film from a good script, but never a good film from a bad one! No matter who your "stars" are.

Is it any wonder the viewers are turning off in droves? Why, if these people at the top are paid so much, why can't they see it?!! What do they <u>do</u> all day? Wankers.

25th Sept.   EXT.   PURGATORY   BEACH

CAST: ME (still the star of my own show – finally, sadly)

Purgatory Beach on a busy day

Surf this morning almost unbelievable. You get waves this perfect only several times a year. No rips. Water temp a divine 20 degrees Celsius. Again the perfect curling breakers. I file away a new idea for a title for something: "The Shape Of Waves". Bit wanky, but still…

Re-read yesterday's rant. Have to admit that collaborative writing is not always a bad experience, or necessarily an exercise in committee-speak or groupthink. Being a small cog in a well oiled story department can be a wonderful, socially enlivening exercise (especially for lonely scribblers like me who mostly work at home). Unfortunately, this is rare, and probably only occurred once in my brilliant career during a short stint on *Something In The Air*. Here at last was a series where writers were actually encouraged to be part of the script development process...

Until somebody pointed out that this involved paying us more money. Then they made sure we were once again spoon fed scene breakdowns - like the writers on every other soapie. Naturally the show collapsed shortly afterwards and a brave new experiment folded amidst the general debacle of what used to be called

'ABC Drama'. It was only a victory for those who know the cost of everything and the value of nothing...

At one stage, a junior editor on *Something In The Air* (who no one would trust with a script), actually got to update the "bible" for the show: a chronicle of names, dates and places that had been added to the fictional landscape after two years on air. A kind of social geography of Emu Springs. It showed that mountains had been named and climbed. That there were valleys, creeks and streams, streets, hospitals, pubs, farms, footy teams, and neighbouring towns- all dreamed up by teams of writers, editors and storyliners. Great wheeling narrative arcs had been set in place that involved the lives and inter-twinings of many scores of individual characters.

No literary artefact on this scale has ever been produced in the history of writing. The average television series or serial is a colossus of collaborative creativity running sometimes to many hundreds of episodes. Of course, certain Victorian novels first appeared in episodic form in popular magazines and ran for months. The work of Dickens, Trollop and Hardy reached a huge, new audience. Nor was illiteracy any barrier, since people could go to "penny readings" where each new instalment was recited out loud. Dickens himself made a fortune from his many live tours.

In the end, however, these works of fiction were published as a single book. Whereas, in a series like *Homicide* or *Blue Heelers* or *Neighbours* with their many episodes, the narrative arc stretches out over the creative equivalent of scores of novels spread out over years or even decades. Now you can buy little novellas of the various *Neighbours* story arcs at any Post Office.

Yet the underlying problem remains... The networks in their eternal struggle for ratings and in the blind panic that accompanies any new series' launch, have lost sight of the very thing they need to cultivate in order to attract an audience in the first place. People will always respond to a show that speaks to some deep, inner truth they all share and can relate to, portraying characters they accept as credible, fallible and familiar. And this only happens when a single 'authorial voice' is in charge.

26th Sept   EXT.   CAPE SURPRISE!

CAST: ME, N/S (Non Speaking) BOARDRIDERS, N/S HANGLIDERS

Sunset Moonrise Cape Surprise!

Cape Surprise!

Enjoying a sunset chardy up at the Cape, sitting on a bench glancing down at the surf a 100 metres below. Where a dilatory, but majestic humpback frolics with her calf in the big rolling swell, heading slowly back to Antarctica. What do whales know or care about how Australian television series get made? What need have they of Scene Breakdowns or Story Arcs. The only arcs they know are the ones they make as they shoot up out of the water before curving back in a massive splash revelling in the sheer joy of being alive.

Not even a dreaded opinion writer can appreciate that the general sequence of events (the "Twelve Step Programme") leading to the creation of an Australian television series is roughly as follows:

Step 1. A network's Head of Drama suddenly gets told by the Programming Department that there's a widening gap in their local content quotas for the upcoming season. They must have a new local series on air, and fast. In the general funk that follows, a patched-together dog of an idea that had been sitting on the back-shelf of the Head of Drama's slush pile is quickly brought forward to much internal fanfare as the next great hope…

Step 2. An intense amount of lunching now takes place. Network credit cards are required to go platinum just to fund the brainstorming sessions at various winebars around the city. Here the basic pub and lounge room sets are planned, designed and ordered, as well as the broad narrative arcs of the dozen or so regular characters with locked-in contracts. A few querky but telegenic locations are thrown into the mix and everyone goes home for a well earned post-prandial nap.

Step 3. All the guys on the board (the former car salesmen and shopping centre property developers who actually own the network – and they are all guys) declare they love it immediately… and by the way if it doesn't rate it's socks off from the pilot episode on, the Head of Drama better start looking round for a Noosa or Port Douglas travel/accommodation package that could incorporate some career counselling and personal re-development time.

Step 4. The shit really starts hitting the fan when the Casting Department suddenly discover that no actor worth their salt is going to commit to three years of emotional compression on a soapie that might go to 11pm after the first series.

Step 5. The panic spreads from the upper echelons of the network's Drama Department (via the consultants, mates and script executives) down to some lucky/unlucky local producer who submitted that dog of an idea and now gets the wake up call that s/he's got about two weeks to cobble together a production office and commission the sets- along with cast, crew, locations and oh yes, scripts for their brilliant idea. The local producer is in a state of shock because s/he hasn't even looked at that submission for over 18 months - when s/he got the last knockback and decided it wasn't worth wasting any more time on.

Step 6. Writers who can remain sober before lunchtime are dragged away from their afternoon schooners and offered a chance to get their first episode on the show just right. Various proposed "active (sic) writers lists" are emailed between the Head of Drama in Sydney and the producers in Melbourne and promptly rejected by Sydney. This usually means that the soon to be appointed trainee script editors will have about two days to rewrite all the first drafts.

Step 7. Meanwhile, a pilot is rushed into production that everyone hopes will pass muster at the test screenings in the Market Researcher's basement laboratory in South Melbourne. Here a small sample of the target audience, like an advertisers' jury, is asked to sit and pass judgement on the work-in-progress. Upon their fickle, brainless, uninformed response hangs the final commitment of money. But by now everyone already knows the series is going to be a dreadful flop because the writers have finally been allowed to view the audition tapes of the actors who got the major roles and they're uniformly hopeless.

Step 8. In order to facilitate the gruelling, 4 hours-a-week, on-air serial production target (to fill the local content quota and get the Network out of a big fine and massive bad publicity), the nucleus of a Story Department is formed and collectively it must quickly furnish the huge outpouring of words required to keep the production crew in constant motion by fleshing out the first 39 episodes (equivalent to about 30 hours of drama, given every episode has about 15 minutes of ads). Thus, in order to speed up the scriptwriting process and save both time and money, the essential business of plotting the show is umbilically separated from the drafting of dialogue and choreographing of movement that must follow.

Step 9. And this is where things start to seriously unravel. A fatal split occurs as two separate writing entities are established: one, a bunch of storyliners, researchers, script co-ordinators and editor/negotiators who are in-house, relatively job secure, and required to turn up for work everyday - where they proceed to sit around big whiteboards and start mapping out the story arcs of the series or serial before them (no one ever quite decides whether it is a series or a serial).

Step 10. The other writing entity is a loose collection of shambolic freelancers with addictive personalities who work singly at home like pieceworkers in the mini word-factory of their own private studios. These are the dialoguists (formerly writers) who must invent the speeches to go with the absurd scenarios handed down to them by the in-house team above - while seamlessly and simultaneously stitching together the gaping holes in their silly plotlines.

Step 11. The writers are handed their contract and small down payment at the 'Scene Breakdown Conference' where their status is now so low they must even pay for their own tea and coffee. (You'd think just once they'd let us go downstairs to the studio and graze across the leftovers of the gourmet feast provided for the crew. But no, that doesn't happen.)

Step 12. The writer/dialoguist's job is to mentally inhabit the given handful of sets and hear the characters speaking (a patently schizophrenic and psychologically damaging process - hence the addictions). But they must always do so within the strict limits of the handed-down scene breakdown.

Yet the process of writing must itself be a journey of discovery or it won't work. The fun and attraction is in the detours and what you find when the plot breaks down. (Which it always does). To simply follow a sanitised, unchangeable road map is to produce an efficient progression from A to B, but it's an experience of travel that, for the audience at least, remains predictable and completely underwhelming.

And this is how everything gets blanded out.

27^h Sep. EXT.   CAFÉ CELESTIAL
ME, N/S LOCAL ARTISTS, N/S CHANNELERS , N/S HEALERS

View from the Café Celestial

I'm sitting at the Café Celestial across from the clock tower on Salvation Strand with its provocative but understandable graffiti and it's colourfully inaccurate depiction of the right time. Just finishing another of Max's (the barista's) excellent skinny caps. Today's workload over by 10.30 am. Picked up *Nirvana News* to find that local producers are mounting a counter attack on behalf of Our Industry. Of course they claim they haven't got the money to compete with the enormous sums thrown at American series (imported by local Networks at a massive discount). But whenever in the history of 'motion pictures' (sic) did high production values guarantee an audience? Look at *Young Lions,* look at *Alice, Water Rats, Dogs Head Bay.*

The chief failure of any drama is always to be found not in the size of the budget but in the quality of the story. The only hope is soap. But why <u>can't</u> television serials be more intelligent and sophisticated?

Next, we'll get directors telling us that they aren't given enough opportunities, actors that they have no continuity of employment, and crews that the lunches have gone down hill. They're all only waiting for the feature break that will get them to Hollywood and out of here. Traitors.

<u>Sept 28th EXT.</u> <u>PEARLY GATES HOTEL</u>
ME, N/S DRINKERS, N/S BAKPAKAHS

Magnificent Mt. Lookout!

Sitting with an excellent Hunter Valley chardy in the Pearly Gates' beer garden, enjoying another rainbow-clad sunset over Mt Lookout, realising (yet again!) that scriptwriting is no career for slackers. Gold and silver coins lie spread across the table in front of me. Just enough for another glass.

I realize now there's little praise, or appreciation of our work as writers. What you finally see on air hardly resembles anything you handed in at second draft. At best I might recognise one or two lines of dialogue. All my brilliant wit and Irish turn of phrase neutered by some twenty-something kid with the life experience of a phytoplankton.

Most Australian teledramatists are proficient, hard-working, funny, zany, mad but dedicated artists. The main problem is - we just don't get to tell our own stories anymore. There are so many points of control and filtering out of anything different or odd. The chances of some individual voice emerging from the whole exercise is approximately zero.

Can't the opinion writers see it? Are they so blind? What pitiful excuses for journalists they are! The thing that's wrong with Australian television is that most of it isn't Australian! It's American. American franchises and British costume drama. That's Australian television. This is not only true in terms of hours of drama put to air, but in the way that 'local' shows imitate American styles. It's why there's so many Cops and Doctors. Why crime and bad health have become the dramatic staples of the hollywoodised, televisual world. All because it's easier to plot. In a crime or an illness the drama is built in. It's lazy writing. Only the soaps with their settings in a community (prison, village, apartment block, suburb, school room) and their mapping of the vagaries of the human heart, offer any kind of hope for something real to break through.

As Raymond Williams clearly saw thirty years ago (in *Television- Technology And Cultural Form*)... "more drama is watched in a single weekend by today's average viewer than most people, through most of human history, would have seen in their entire lifetime."

Modern humans are saturated with drama. Our consciousness is altered by the sheer amount of synthetic human behaviour that we consciously or unconsciously observe. So what are we doing to this enormous audience !? Why can't our local industry be the shining light that shows people how to behave nobly, generously, charitably towards each other? Why must our teledrama always be so violent, so negative, so destructive? I ask without getting any satisfactory answer...

29ᵗʰ Sept. EXT.   LIMBO CREEK
CAST: ME (alone again, unfortunately)

Lovely Limbo Creek

Lovely Limbo Creek meets Purgatory Beach

Gave myself a "Day Off" today, a well earned rest between segments for the current episode of *On Golden Sands*. Spent mainly sunbaking on the dunes where Limbo Creek meets Purgatory Beach. The malaise continues…Wasted last night watching Channel 9's *50 Years/50 Shows-* celebrating five decades of Australian Television. I am told that the second most important series ever made is the *Paul Hogan Show*. Just behind Graham Kennedy's iconic *In Melbourne Tonight*. All comedy and variety. The closest a local drama gets is *Brides Of Christ* at number 5 – just ahead of the *Don Lane Show* but well behind the *Opening Of The Sydney Olympics*. And while I've got nothing against guys who wear tight shorts and footy jerseys with the sleeves cut out, and hang around with a mate who seems to suffer intellectual impairment while constantly wearing a life saver's cap, and while Graham Kennedy was no doubt a very talented man, to discover that these characters are the high water mark of my beloved industry!? No wonder I feel so low. Will need serious lubrication this afternoon.

Oct 2nd EXT.   NULLUMBAH AIRPORT
CAST: ME, N/S PASSENGERS, N/S AIRLINE STAFF

Nullumbah International Airport

Busy Nullumbah Airport

Sitting in the shed that passes for Nullumbah Airport's waiting room - awaiting Rural Air's tiger moth that will take me to another one-day script conference in Sydney for episode 4765 of *On Golden Sands*. Tomorrow I will be handed another blanded out Scene Breakdown that I must find the dialogue for. Dialogue that will be quickly rewritten as soon as I hand it in. Why don't I just shoot myself and end the misery now? Perhaps the moth will crash and save me the trouble.

More depressing news as I gaze in vacant wonderment at the national tabloids. Another bombing outrage in Bali. The 'War' on Horrorism continues as we're told that more of our basic human rights will have to be shed in the interests of 'security'- whatever that is.

The great George Orwell saw it coming when he predicted in *1984* that "the 'War' will be eternal." That there will always be a threat we must arm ourselves against. It's how the elites maintain control. There is a sickness loose upon the world. And its us! Life is a sexually transmitted disease. And it's terminal! I started in this business believing, like Genet, that every writer must be fired with a burning desire to change the world...So much for youthful idealism.

Later, in the plane flying south, listening to *Late Night Live* on my complimentary headphones, I recall that Phillip Adams once famously asked: "Has it really been 25 years of Australian Television or just the same year over and over again?"

Now another 25 years have passed since his cheeky remark. And I ask the same question. Has it really been <u>50</u> years of Australian Television or <u>still</u> the same year over and over again?

No- that's just too paranoid. And depressing (if its true).
If word got out I thought like that I'd never work for a Network again...

Paul Davies is best known for his location theatre work (including *Storming Mont Albert By Tram*) and first discovered the exciting connection between pretending and public funding when he won one pound in a smiling competition at the Vogue Picture Theatre, Ipswich in 1956. He has since kept audiences mildly amused through eight plays (mostly for TheatreWorks), six documentaries, two features and too many scripts on a dozen different television series- from *Homicide* to *The Sullivans* and more recently *Something In The Air* and *Stingers.*

KILLING *HOMICIDE*
(The Demise Of A Cultural Icon)
Paul Davies
METRO #149 (2006)

The Last "Gang of Four"
Top: Bud Tingwell, Dennis Grosvenor
Bottom: Don Barker, Gary Day

HOMICIDE

Initially rejected by the Nine Network, *Homicide* was made by Crawford Productions for Channel Seven where it enjoyed an unbroken, twelve year run from 1964 to 1975, achieving a total production slate of 510 hour-length episodes. This enduring success, with consistently high ratings, helped establish the viability of Australian television drama generally. *Homicide* was compared to Britain's *Z Cars* and America's *Naked City*. Its local roots were Crawford's earlier police radio drama *D24*, and the courtroom-based *Consider Your Verdict*. *Homicide*'s low budget constraints were innovatively deployed to replicate a certain gritty, suburban realism. Plots were taken from real life cases. Chases were more on foot than by car. Stunts were done by the actors themselves. An early decision to clearly acknowledge the location as Melbourne enhanced its appeal with local viewers who, amidst a plethora of imported product, were seeing their own streets and backyards, and hearing their own vernacular represented on the small screen for the first time. The original cast of John Fegan, Terry McDermott and Lex Mitchell were soon joined by Leonard Teale (Sen. Det. David 'Mac' Mackay) who became the squad's longest serving detective, making a special re-appearance for the final episode ("The Last Task"). Other key actors in a rotating squad of three or four, included Alwyn Kurts, John Stanton and 'Bud' Tingwell. Later episodes were shot entirely on 16mm film, allowing greater access to both exterior and interior locations. Fashioned within the show's fixed narrative structure (of murder, investigation, arrest – all viewed strictly from the police point of view) these final episodes became effectively short (42 minute) features, providing an apt training ground for many of the key players in the Australian New Wave film movement that followed *Homicide*'s demise in 1975. These included directors George Miller, Simon Wincer, David Stevens, Kevin Dobson and Igor Auzins, as well as screenwriters Keith Thompson, Peter Schreck, Phil Friedman, Cliff Green and Everett de Roche.

From *A Companion to the Australian Media*
(Macquarie University 2014)
Paul Davies

Although I didn't realise it at the time, in 1975 I was effectively the last script editor on the classic Aussie cop show, *Homicide*. Around May news filtered down that the Network, unhappy with the way things were going, had just cancelled the last eight scripts! Ones that I had just released for production. This was an unprecedented intrusion into a show's executive independence, especially one that had been in continuous and successful motion for eleven years.

And, although the ratings were down from the stratospheric fifties and forties of its golden period, *Homicide* was still garnering the kind of audience numbers that producers today would rejoice over (and probably take the entire production staff out to lunch for). It was unheard of for Channel Seven to actually *read* a release draft of any *Homicide* script, let alone *cancel* eight in a row!

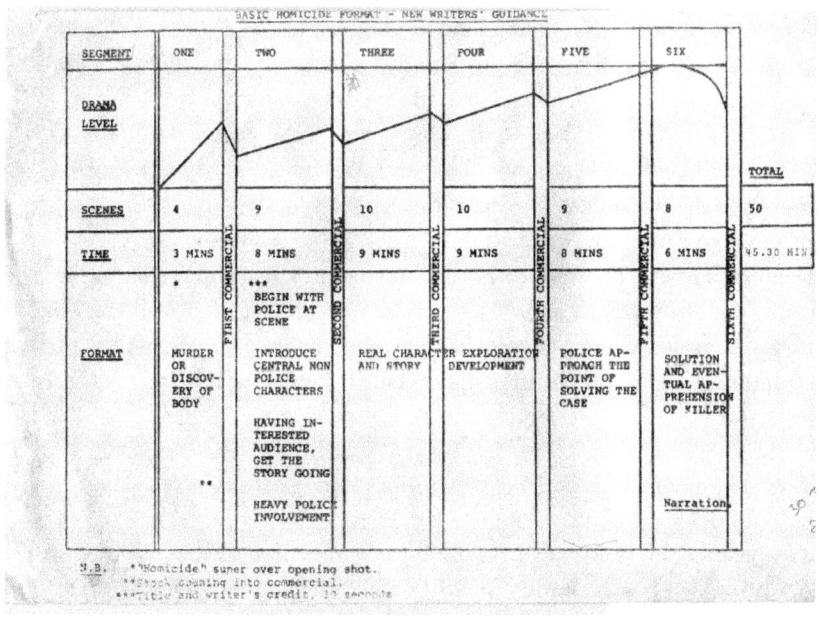

How to write a Homicide script.
The basic template

The above graph shows the classic Homicide/teledrama structure given to all writers on the show: starting with the discovery of the body in the opening three minute 'teaser', and then building DRAMA LEVEL up through four ad breaks and on to the climax of the murderer's capture in the second last segment. Followed by a summary of his conviction and gaol sentence. Always seeing everything from the police point of view.

The crisis of eight cancelled scripts meant, of course, that some lowly, blamable entity (namely the current script editor), would have to concoct an 'acceptable' replacement script in less than three days - simply in order to keep the show's sixty five permanent staff in some semblance of gainful employment.

Alas, Episode 511:*"Double Take"*, the last ever *Homicide*, co-written by Adrian Davies-Moore (a plainly fanciful name) and directed by the remarkable Igor Auzins, didn't save the series. Shortly afterwards, the dreaded Network guillotine fell, and a brave experiment in local teledrama was over.

So who murdered the men in pork pie hats? And why did they have such narrow brims when the whole idea of a hat is to keep the sun off?

The simple answer is: Network 7 killed the nation's flagship drama series. They wielded the sharp implement. (This was an axe murder after all). But why did such a successful, cutting edge, local teledrama have to die so swiftly and with such little ceremony ? Like an embarrassment, instead of the great achievement it was.

In the tradition of any good *Homicide* script, we must start with the body:

Eleven years old is positively geriatric for any television series. A certain senility takes over about year seven (look at *Blue Heelers, Neighbours, Home And Away*). The formula just runs out of puff. Yet *Homicide* had been able to keep re-inventing itself through many changes to the core cast (15 detectives in all) and constant technological upgrading (from clunky three-camera black and white video in a couple of studio sets to highly portable 16mm colour film shot on locations all over Melbourne). In it's final incarnation, each episode of the show was approached almost like an auteured mini-feature.

Actors of the calibre of John Hargreaves, Noni Hazelhurst, Pamela Stephenson and Simon Chilvers were taking major guest roles. And many later feature directors like George Miller, Simon Wincer, David Stevens, Paul Eddy and Igor Auzins, cut their directorial teeth on these final *Homicide* episodes.

Some, like Kevin Dobson with *Long Weekend*, were inventing their own film style, in this case a grainy, Ken Loachy kind of look to carry Keith Thompson's taut little love story about a troubled teenager (Noni Hazelhurst) and her tragic low-life boyfriend (John Geros). Along with three other contemporary episodes, *Long Weekend* was deemed unsuitable for screening before 8.30pm by the Broadcasting Control Board, further jeopardizing *Homicide's* place in the Network schedule.

In *Free Enterprise* George Miller told the story of a group of residents, including some communists, who took on a corrupt government bureaucracy in order to halt the re-development of their street. In John Drew's *Why All The Fuss* the show literally lived up its often misspelt title '*Homocide*' when the boys in pork pie hats found Doug Lambert (Grigor Taylor) bashed and bleeding from a vicious homophobic attack. In another episode by John Drew called *Charlie,* Drew tackled the twin minefields of mental illness and paedophilia. Other stories were concerned with child abuse (*The Life And Times Of Tina Kennedy)*, abortion, and murders that occur as a result of the aggression inherent in excessive alcohol consumption - stuff that didn't go down terribly well with some of the Networks major advertisers, particularly large corporations involved in the brewing of hops.

What Channel Seven wanted was good, clean, plain-old family oriented detective work where the principal cast - the 'gang of four'- were the major focus and the audience could never be allowed to get ahead of them by discovering what the crims were up to first.

But for any writer struggling with the rigid *Homicide* format, (see the graph of the 'basic template' above) the guest characters were the ones you got to make up yourself. Plus, there was now a greater opportunity to spread the storytelling. Under the aegis of producers like Igor Auzins, Paul Eddy and Henry Crawford, the *Homicide* writers could basically tackle any issue they liked. Subjects they were passionate about. Luis Bayonas, being Spanish, always wrote murders involving blades. Jim Simmonds could be counted on to do something with a sport – usually the martial arts. John Drew tackled the hard social stuff. As did Keith Thompson and Peter Shreck.

Yet on the18th June 1975, attempting to stem the rot, and running up the surrender flag, Hector Crawford announced in an All Staff Memo, that Igor Auzins was being replaced as producer by Don Battye. In the *TV Times* two weeks later, Mr. Battye was quoted as saying the show had become "sensational, and too involved in social issues. We've got to get back to the basic idea and that's murder". In a 7.30 time slot. Suitable for family viewing- goes without saying.

But even this didn't work because the axe kept falling and soon sixty five people (along with many other contracted artists) were out of a job. Within a several months Crawfords' other cop shows, *Division 4* and *Matlock Police* were also cast into the dust bin of history.

It looked like payback. Crawford Productions had not only proven that local teledrama could find and keep an audience, but had actively campaigned on behalf of local content through its backing of the *TV Make It Australian Committee* - continuing a fight that stretched back to the company's bid for the license of Australia's third commercial channel- the 0/10 Network in 1964, the year *Homicide* started.

At that time Hector Crawford pushed forward the staggering idea that this proposed new network should be a 'local content only' affair. An unheard of proposition that threatened to set a bad example for the free flow (flood, tidal wave) of American and British product onto our small screens. Not surprisingly, Hector lost out to Reg Ansett in that bid for 0/10, and 11 years later, Crawford Productions was brought to its knees by the sudden cancellation of three quarters of it's cash flow. A move that seemed to culturally pre-empt the larger destabilization and eventual dismissal of the Whitlam Government in Canberra five months later.

The Box - itself an almost documentary account of what went on in the company- kept Crawfords on a respirator through the lean months of late '75 and early '76, until *The Sullivans* once again produced a mega hit for Ian Jones and Henry Crawford, thus ensuring the company's survival for the next half decade.

Is eleven years long enough for a series to be on air?

Probably. But *Homicide* was breaking new ground, dealing with tough social and political issues and still finding a respectably large enough sized audience.

The show had started, like it's radio predecessor *D24,* as something made for and with the full co-operation of the Victorian Police Force - who obviously saw it as great PR. Indeed, in the early days, innocent bystanders, not recognizing a film crew, would dive in and try to rescue stunt dummies from crashed cars. But by 1975 the show was dealing with a much more complex approach to law and order. Something the police hierarchy were obviously less interested in being associated with. It clouded the message.

Were there too many cop shows on Australian television at the time?

Undoubtedly. But what else is new ? Cops, Doctors and Soaps are the staples.

Was there a cultural conspiracy to stifle local content by bringing down it's principle flag bearer ?

Who knows? And, without going undercover, like *Homicide's* offspring *Stingers*, how could you ever prove it ? In this sense it also mirrors the problem of the larger destabilisation of the Whitlam Government. There will never be a smoking gun (police issue .32 calibre).

Only one thing is certain: in mid- 1975 there was a decision made to terminate Australia's first really successful drama series at a moment when it had become a fascinating experiment in expressive filmmaking. As an incurable hippy romantic, one pipe dream I still have relates to how Australia might have found itself today if the Crawford and Whitlam cultural and political agendas had been allowed to win through and flourish.

I imagine an impossibly clever, confidant and benevolent society with real economic, racial and gender equality. One that still has free tertiary education, universal health cover, a viable social security net, respect for Native Title, and a publicly owned banking, telecommunications and transport infrastructure.

I also imagine such a society would almost certainly have a film and teledrama industry that was at the cutting edge of world entertainment; yet one which still gave a voice to it's own community, always breaking new ground, and ready to celebrate every kind of local hero (with or without a pork pie hat).

Oh well, I said it was a dream...

Logie winning director Igor Auzins, left, in action.

so long against the has entered in the TV

Penultimate *Homicide* producer Igor Auzins in action on Episode 474 *"Why All the Fuss"* written by John Drew – a gay bashing story shot around Hector Crawford's home swimming pool. On June 18th 1975 Auzins was replaced by Don Battye who called for less "sensationalism and social issues" and more murder.

Mr FRED BETTS (right) addresses the demonstration at City Square, Melbourne. From left, Gerard Kennedy, Terry Donovan.

800 TV people in protest
march for more local shows

MORE than 800 actors : "We have tried to put our programs like Upstairs, Down- realised the 75 per cent local

"Life imitating art imitating life: Fred Betts (who played the Hector Crawford character in *The Box)* rousing the masses to action to defend local content on Australian TV. In the background, Lieutenants Gerard Kennedy and Terry Donovan (Jason's dad) both playing cops on *Division 4* – another hugely successful Crawfords police procedural - stand by for crowd control, ready to draw on their extensive combined acting experience playing both crims *and* detectives)

SOMETHING IN THE STORYLINE
(Finding the "Author" in Serial Teledrama)

Paul Davies
"Works In Progress" Conference
University of Queensland, Brisbane (August 24-25 2012)

Something In The Air, a rural soap opera set around a country radio station in the declining but fictional town of 'Emu Springs', screened four nights a week at 6pm on ABC television from January 2000 to May 2002. This was commonly understood as the '*Bellbird*' time slot and was designed to deliver the ABC's heartland audience, the 'grey cardigan brigade' (and others), into the 7pm news. *SITA* won an AFI award for the best Australian Drama series in 2001, and ran to a total of 320 half-hour episodes. Despite its serial nature, each episode was given an individual title and the original 'bible' for the show invited writers to have 'significant input at storyline stage' and then take 'the screenplay through to second draft'. While welcoming the unusual amount of creative freedom being offered, in mid 2000 the writers took the *SITA* producers (Beyond Simpson Le Measurier) to Arbitration, arguing that they were being denied 25% of the base fee due to them for creative input into the 'storyline'. The producers countered that they did in fact "provide writers with a fully developed storyline". In his judgment, the Hon. R.J Garlick found "broadly in favour" of the writers and ordered that they be back-paid the requisite 25%. Taking as a case study one episode of *SITA* written by myself (Block 9, Episode 33, *Rotten Eggs*), this paper seeks to use the issues raised by this industrial dispute as a lens for examining and unpacking the complex web of creative inter-relationships that necessarily take place in the production of scripts for long running television series. These are narrative artefacts that can now spin out to hundreds and thousands of hours of scripted drama. The paper briefly outlines the structure of a typical, contemporary 'script department' such as the one operating on *SITA*, and touches on questions of *originality, appropriation* and *interdependence* in such an intensely *collaborative* and *creative* working environment - one which effectively industrializes the role of author. *Rotten Eggs* and its sequel episode, *Return Of The Prodigal* (Episode 34) were awarded an AWGIE (Australian Writer's Guild Award) for the best 'TV Serial' scripts in 2000.

Something in the Storyline
Defining the Author and Negotiating the Narrative in 'serial teledrama'.

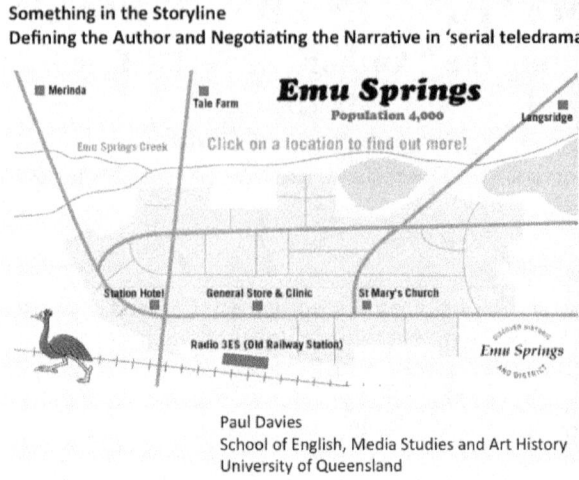

Paul Davies
School of English, Media Studies and Art History
University of Queensland

This paper examines the nature of authorship in the production of scripts for the ABC series *Something In The Air* (*SITA*) which screened across 320 episodes from January 2000 to May 2002.

As such, it is more a work-long-finished than a "work-in-progress" but it's a story I've wanted to tell in some way for a long time and it seemed to me to be a neat fit for the conference themes of *originality* and *authorship* as it specifically here as it relates to writing television drama - something which necessarily involves the *mixing* and *sharing* of creative roles in an increasingly deconstructed and diversified writing process.

This is not an argument about or against collaboration. Personally, I'm very happy to share the writing process with fellow actors, directors or script editors, being a playwright or scriptwriter can be much more fun than being a solitary poet or novelist stuck at home in the garret. And in any case, in television you have to leave the authorial ego behind. A relentless production machine dictates that you are inevitably part of an extended team.

It also poses the questions: where does collaboration end and appropriation of the role of author begin? Does "groupthink" necessarily lead to a kind of industrialization of the creative function?

And it is strange to be asking these questions here now, looking back on a body of work that was the direct outcome of my being here (at the University of Queensland) as a student in the first place, reading the Great Tradition of English literature and being seduced by the drama side into a career writing for performance across a number of platforms. To that extent 'the work' is ongoing. It is a work-in-progress that only finishes when I do.

THE ROLE OF THE SCRIPTWRITER

The tendency to systematize the role of the scriptwriter can be seen in the earliest forms of Australian television drama including the foundational police series *Homicide* which ran to 510 one hour episodes from 1964 to 1975. Here the requisite emotional template ('Drama Level') for a typical *Homicide* story was laid out graphically in the *Homicide* bible:

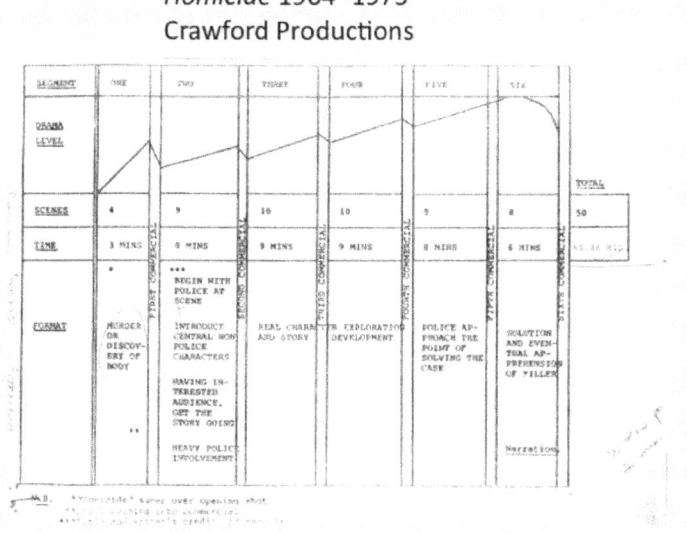

Emotional 'flow chart' of a typical episode across six segments

This graph describes a narrative arc of building 'emotional intensity' across six segments of action running to a total of (more or less) 50 scenes across exactly 45 minutes of screen time. This Leaves room for 15 minutes of ads in the so called TV hour (sic). A *Homicide* episode almost invariably begins with the discovery of the body in the short, 3 minute "teaser" at the beginning of the episode and follows the step by step police investigation of the murder, to the "eventual apprehension of the killer".

Obviously, the need for a large number of scripts to service the production of an on-going television series requires not only an in-house 'Script Department' but also a number of freelance writers – all working to a particular set of guidelines relating to genre, style, character, physical location, historical setting, budget etc.

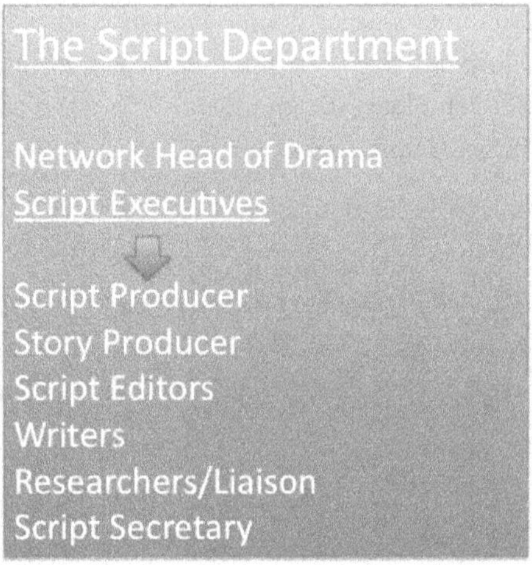

The Script Department

Network Head of Drama
Script Executives

Script Producer
Story Producer
Script Editors
Writers
Researchers/Liaison
Script Secretary

The Script Department hierarchy

Here the Script Department (producers, story editors, script editors, consultants and researchers), are responsible for the original "story engine," as Roger Simpson of Beyond Simpson Le Mesurier (BSLM) described it. This is the dramatic combination of characters, setting, style and themes that drives the series as a whole. It allows for the broad narrative arc of the series to be mapped out and mined for individual stories.[1] The writers work within this story engine (and the regular characters available for their episode) to produce an initial 'storyline' before proceeding to an intermediary 'scene breakdown' stage. Finally, various drafts containing detailed action and dialogue are written (usually two) and these are then timed and finalized by the script editors before being 'released' to the director and their production crew (who in turn may produce a shooting draft that can then be scheduled and budgeted).

[1] "Looking For The Story Engine, Breakfast with Roger Simpson" *Metro* 135 (2003): 186-195. Print.

The most salient point of intersection of this authorial binary of macro storytelling and micro character development therefore is to be found in the initial, original storyline.[2]

The background information to a series (characters, setting, story engine, style, genre etc.) is supplied in the form of a 'writer's bible'.

Something In The Air
Writers' Bible
1999

Outlines: Setting, Characters, Story Approach, 'Logistical Information', Available Sets/Locations, Research etc.

As part of its 'logistical information' section, the original bible for *SITA* invited writers to provide 'significant input at storyline stage'.[3] and this clause became crucial in the industrial dispute that occurred in March 2000 between the Australian Writer's Guild (AWG) and the Screen Producers Association of Australia (SPPA) over what exactly constituted a 'storyline' for *SITA*. This was especially important given that the provision of such was equivalent to 25% of MBUF (Minimum Basic Use Fee).[4] In the "Series and Serials Agreement" (SASA)

---

[2] In some series such as *Neighbours* and *Home and Away* the writer is provided with an already completed scene breakdown and paid only for the draft (s).

[3] Beyond Simpson Le Mesurier. *Something In The Air.* "Writer's Bible" Melbourne: ABC, 1999. Print.

[4] In the standard *SITA* contract at this time the Minimum Basic Use Fee (MBUF) was $2,186.88 for a half hour episode of which $546.72 was deducted for the storyline. With additional remuneration for repeats, foreign rights, attendance at the story conference and a 'personal margin' (of $1355.07), the total income to a writer for a single, half hour *SITA* episode in 2000 was $5,048.07.

on which the *SITA* writer's contracts were drawn up, the storyline was defined as the "written synopsis of the story in narrative form, providing sufficient detail so that the essential dramatic development and main characters can be identified, and from which the writer can develop the scene breakdown."[5]

The Storyline

* Most basic narrative outline

* Establishes the "Beats" in the Story

(Beats = Key Moments of Action)

* Demonstrates: Set- Up
                         Conflict
                         Resolution

SPAA (the Screen Producers Association of Australia), on behalf of BSLM (Beyond Simpson Le Measurier), argued in the Arbitration hearing that the *SITA* script department *were* providing the "written synopsis of the story in narrative form" prior to the initial story conference for each Block (of four episodes) and therefore had the right to deduct 25% of the fee otherwise due to the writer.

The AWG Australian Writer's Guild, on behalf of the writers, argued that what BSLM called a "storyline" was essentially only a set of "pre-plot notes" in point form, and in any case the writers contributed to the basic "narrative" through their active participation in the story conference that initiated each Block.[6]

In his judgment, the Hon. R. J. Garlick found "broadly in favour of the writers" and ordered that they be back-paid the requisite 25%. However his honour made the following significant observations:

---

[5] The definition is quoted in Garlick, Hon. R.J. "The Australian Writers' Guild and the Screen Producers Association of Australia" Decision. 19.6. 2000.

[6] According to a submission from *SITA* writer Ysabelle Dean "If the storyline is the document that came out of the two day plotting meetings, I contributed very heavily to its creation… the notes provided to me before the meetings [were] simply a loose collection of pre-plot ideas with which to get the ball rolling." (Paul Davies Script Archive, Fryer Library, University of Queensland, Brisbane).

This has serious practical implications... For the Producer consideration has to be given as to whether they wish to have in-house writers clearly writing a Storyline and not expecting writers at a Story Conference to do more than listen and offer views and suggestions. In the latter situation writers of course would have to accept that they did not have a *recognised creative role in writing the Storyline...* it is difficult to be didactic, let alone legal, about *identifiable phases in that process.* The reality may be that *the basic structure of the creative writing process* envisaged by SASA, that is Storyline, Scene Breakdown, First Draft, Final Draft, *is no longer meeting the realities of the production needs.* (emphasis added)[7]

SOMETHING IN THE AIR (2000- 2002)

Something In The Air 1999-2002
ABC and Beyond Simpson Le Mesurier

L-R (standing) Tom, Joe, Ryan, (unknown) Julia, Doug, Mon.
(sitting) Helen, Harry, Sally, Megan, Dr. Anne, Wayne.

The regular (recurring) characters of *SITA,* First series (2000).

The realities of the production needs of *SITA* were quite stark. Basically, four half-hours of television drama were produced every five working days requiring almost twenty minutes of screen time to be shot per day, using a handful of sets (radio station, pub, general store and the living rooms of two farm houses) in a barely

---

[7] Garlick, Hon. R.J.. Decision. 19.6.2000

sound-proof studio.[8] Such a schedule allows little time to do more than one take of any particular shot, and puts considerable strain on all aspects of the creative process from story concept through to finished 'deliverables'.

SITA was based around a radio station in 'Emu Springs', a small, fictional town with a gold mining past and a declining population. It screened at 6pm on the ABC network in what was commonly understood as the 'Bellbird' time slot and was clearly designed to deliver the ABC's heartland audience, the 'grey cardigan brigade' (and others), into the 7pm news.

Preview article connecting *Something In the Air* with *Bellbird*

Block 9, Episode 33, "Rotten Eggs"
(Director: Richard Jascek, Producer: Roz Tatarka, Writer: Paul Davies)

In the case of my first episode "Rotten Eggs" [9] the theme for the week was to be initially, "Letting Go", and then "Beliefs" both of which related to the imminent demise of Len Taylor (played by Ray Barrett).

---

[8] An additional constraint on the storytelling process was the limited number of guest roles available (one or two per block) plus the contractual complexities resulting from different actors being available for only one, two or three episodes per week.

[9] Originally I was commissioned to write two episodes of 'Block 10' but an earlier block of episodes had 'fallen over' and were dumped so Block 10 became 9 in the running order.

Something to dream on

A show based around a rural community radio station is the ABC's big hope. By **Debi Enker**

Great expectations: Ray Barrett and Anne Phelan, on Len and Mon Taylor, are just two of the homely characters.

Mon and Len Taylor   (Ray Barrett and Anne Phelan)

Ray Barrett ('Len Taylor') Anne Phelan ('Mon Taylor')
Owners and operators of the Emu Springs general store.
(Len's exit from Emu Springs formed the narrative basis for Episode 33)

Nothing incites the creative energies of a script department quite like the removal or introduction of a major character. Block Nine provided both. But Len Taylor's exit had long been prepared for by failing health (irritatingly persistent bouts of coughing) and deep personal shame over his son, Wayne's imprisonment for 'car jacking'.[10] Wayne is a superb footballer and Len the coach of the local team ("the Emus") who have virtually never won a game.

It was almost pre-ordained therefore, that Len's final exit from Emu Springs would coincide with Wayne's surprise return (Episode 34 "Return of the Prodigal")

---

[10] Ray Barrett had only agreed to join the show on a limited basis and so his death was prepared for from day one of the series. This was unlike Eric Bana's sudden exit to make Ridley Scott's *Black Hawk Down,* which resulted in a quick switch of actors playing the Joe Sabatini role from Bana to Vince Colossimo. In this case the script department, given the entrenched nature of television production, was unable to incorporate such a sudden exit within an already pre-determined narrative arc.

framed by a bitter/sweet moment of triumph for the 'Emus' over their bitter rivals the Bullandra 'Bulls'.

In 'teledrama' parlance this was the 'A Story'. The 'B Story' (which can have its own narrative thread, but must also relate back to the overall theme), invoked memories of the death of another father: young Harry's dad, Warwick, tragically killed in a car accident some years prior to the show's narrative start date and who, therefore, we have never seen (except here as a ghost).

An additional 'C Story' revolved around the father/daughter contest between single dad and local publican, Stuart McGregor, and his growing concerns over the social habits of his daughter Megan, a young radio announcer on 3ES. The studio set for this local radio station is, along with the pub set, the main hub of action in the show, with characters constantly turning up and passing through both. Megan. as the publican's daughter, is of course central to both.

Megan McGregor
(Mariel McClory)
Trainee Radio
Announcer/
Casual Barmaid

THE AWG/SPPA STORYLINE DISPUTE.

Two parts – the A and B stories of this tripartite narrative scaffolding was first outlined in the 'pre-plot notes' for Block 9 supplied to me by the *SITA* script department and summarized in eight sentences.

The pre-plot notes supplied for Block 9 (Episodes 33, 34, 35, 36) by BSLM are as follows:

---

1. "Beliefs": *The final footy game of the year is imminent and LEN wants to go out with a win.*

2. TOM indulges himself with anti-football views while HELEN tries to provide what consolation she can to HARRY who is having to face the reality that his old mate LEN is teetering towards the big black hole.

3. When LEN and MON'S son, WAYNE, returns to be with his father, LEN realizes the footy team is in with a chance. WAYNE is not only a great player but also a major hunk who causes female knees to tremble wherever he goes, despite an obscure recent past.

4. But there's unfinished business between WAYNE and his parents which has to be resolved.

5. And unfinished business as well between HELEN and HARRY to do with Warwick's passing.

6. As the final siren sounds on the day of the great match, the Emu's are in front. LEN'S ticker, however, gives way in the excitement but he dies a happy man.

7. FATHER BRIAN helps MON deal with her loss while HARRY has already arranged for LEN to take a personal message to his dad.

8. As the rest of the town celebrates LEN'S life and their great victory on the field, HELEN comes to terms with Warwick's death and dances a slow tango with his ghost before finally letting him go.

In BSLM's view the above document constituted a 'storyline' for the purposes of the SPAA/AWG industrial agreement (SASA).

Basic storyline provided for Episodes 33, 34,35,36
    B STORY: A STORY: (No C STORY at this stage)

"Beliefs": The final footy game of the year is imminent and LEN wants to go out with a win

TOM indulges himself with anti-football views
While HELEN tries to provide what consolation she can to HARRY
    who is having to face the reality that his old mate
    LEN is teetering towards the big black hole.
When LEN and MON'S son, WAYNE, returns to be with his father,
    LEN realises the footy team is in with a chance.
    WAYNE is not only a great player
    but also a major hunk who causes female knees to tremble wherever he goes,
    despite an obscure recent past.
    But there's unfinished business between WAYNE and his parents which has to be resolved.
And unfinished business as well between HELEN and HARRY to do with Warwick's passing.
As the final siren sounds on the day of the great match, the Emu's are in front.
    LEN'S ticker, however, gives way in the excitement but he dies a happy man.
FATHER BRIAN helps MON deal with her loss
While HARRY has already arranged for LEN to take a personal message to his dad.
As the rest of the town celebrates LEN'S life and their great victory on the field,
HELEN comes to terms with Warwick's death
    and dances a slow tango with his ghost before finally letting him go.

The question confronted by Justice Garlick was whether these eight sentences amounted to a "written synopsis of the story in narrative form" with "provision of sufficient detail" so that "the *essential* dramatic development and main characters" could "be identified" (emphasis added).

To be fair to BSLM, the eight sentence outline was followed by an additional page of notes in which the A, B and C stories were fleshed out across my two episodes (33 and 34). From these notes, and after a discussion with the Script Department (the story Conference), I was then required to construct a Scene Breakdown for both *Rotten Eggs* (episode 33) and *Return of the Prodigal* (episode 34).

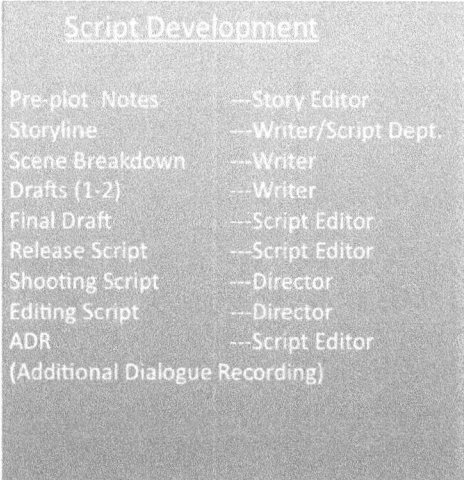

A 'Scene Breakdown' is defined in the SASA as "an outline or synopsis of scenes in narrative form of the entire story indicating the fuller structure and development and characterization of the plot."[11] In "Rotten Eggs" the Scene Breakdown distributes the action outlined in the 8 sentences of the pre-plot notes, via the story conference, across 24 individual scenes, each a paragraph long, which effectively conflates BLSM 'storyline' of around 800 to approximately 6,000 words.[12] After further feedback from the script department (filtering in turn, feedback from the BSLM and the ABC's drama executives) a draft script of around 8,000 words is produced with fully formatted dialogue, scene headings and descriptions of action. If the storyline equates to a poem, and the scene breakdown resembles a short story, the finished draft of a half hour episode might be considered similar to a one act play.[13]

The Hon. R. J. Garlick. found that "[o]n any reasonable reading of the material before me the Writers have made a substantive contribution at the Story

---

[11] Quoted in Garlick, Hon. R.J.. Decision. 19.6.2000

[12] Examples of these and other materials including first and second drafts of these episodes, and DVD copies of the finished product can also be found in Paul Davies Script Archive, Fryer Library, University of Queensland, Brisbane.

[13] The Release Script of Episode 33 was timed at 23 minutes 15 seconds of drama content. Nor does the process of script writing end with this "Release Script". Almost invariably significant additional amendments are made to the "Final Draft" by the in-house script editors as further (sometimes technical) issues arise and director and performer reactions feed through. Even after principal shooting has finished additional dialogue may be required to cover mistakes or problems that occur during the actual shooting. This is called the ADR (Additional Dialogue Recording) script.

Conference [following on from the pre-plot notes] even though it is a contribution [which] cannot be apportioned in exact percentages between them and others." He went on to say that the "...opposed positions of the parties exemplify *the difficulties of assessing the value of contributions to the creative process in sophisticated but meaningful terms* for the purposes of the arcane world of the law of contract" (emphasis added).[14]

It is easy to empathise with his honour's perplexity. The world of compartmentalized authorship he confronted is one in which the threads, once sewn by various parties to the plot (literally) are almost impossible to unravel. In accepting the AWGIE for "Return of the Prodigal" I acknowledged my gratitude to Roger Simpson for "the lend of his characters". To be honest and in retrospect, any working 'teledramatist' could have made a reasonable story out of the pre-plot notes supplied for "Rotten Eggs", but it may not have been in conformity with the over-aching narrative for the show. The issue therefore comes down to narrative control.

Yet as any series grows and develops it necessarily incorporates and processes the input of many dozens of story tellers engaged along a lengthening chain of narrative creation. Characters and events grow in complexity as back stories are added and embellished, and (literally) new territories explored.

COLLECTIVE AUTHORSHIP IN A SHARED IMAGINARY.

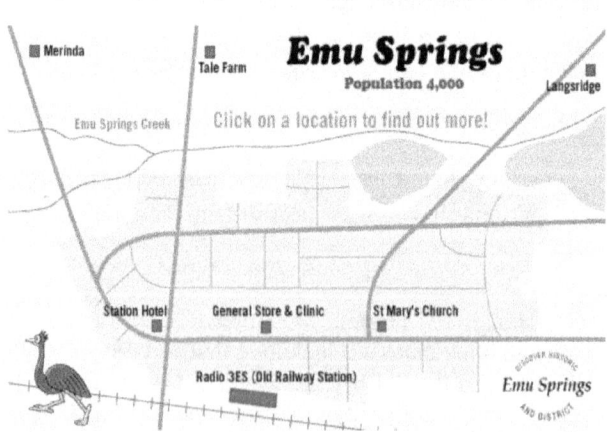

(http://www.abc.net.au/tv/something/ accessed 11/8/2012)[15]

---

[14] Garlick, Hon. R.J.. Decision. 19.6.2000

[15] Only parts of the *SITA* website were accessible on 11/8/2012.

The map in Figure 6 above can now be viewed as a kind of cartographical palimpsest on which the dramatic action of *SITA* unfolded: a starting point to be fleshed out and written upon by a number of writers and editors using additional (guest) characters, with their own back stories and places of abode – locations and events that feed into the burgeoning collective imaginary of the show, something available to all who work on it as much as those who watch the final result.

By the end of the first series of *SITA* it became necessary to consolidate this growing narrative database with a twenty five page 'Scripted Guide to Emu Springs' containing updates on the main characters, including their families, friends and associates, as well as an evolving 'history' of the town, its main businesses, social clubs, ritual celebrations, neighbouring towns, clan rivalries etc. Such a document can be incorporated into an evolving show bible and in turn becomes the basis for additional stories, by other writers, further down the track.

CONCLUSION:
AWG V SPAA - A PYRRHIC VICTORY?

One outcome of the *SITA* storyline dispute saw a number of writers back-paid for a number of episodes where the pre-plot notes were deemed to be inadequate. However, BSLM and the ABC decided that henceforth the provision of a 'storyline' would be a legally unassailable document and to that extent the writer's basic income from an episode remained unchanged (at around $5000). But of course, it's never about the money, because the *SITA* writers also lost the opportunity to shape individual episodes from their inception as narratives in their most nascent form (the storyline).[16]

Two questions remain: was this a good or bad thing? And when does 'collaboration' tip over into mechanisation of the creative function for the purposes of streamlining and control by an in-house team. After all a storyline has to be paid for one way or another, whether it goes to an individual writer or an in-house team. Curiously, but not surprisingly, the business of storytelling on television needs both its structured and its anarchic elements (plot and character/editor and writer/teams and individuals).

The irony, by way of answer, is that a production which started from a desire to encourage writers into the process of script generation, ended up emphatically

---

[16] In a revised bible for *SITA* the invitation for the writer to have "significant input at storyline stage" was changed to "the storylines will be generated in house".

freezing them out. The initial high hopes were duly acknowledged in *SITA*'s first year with an AFI award for best Australian series. In critic, Simon Hughes' words, *SITA*'s "not inconsiderable achievement" was to couch "hard matter within the airy nothing of a nightly soap".[17] Corrie Perkin also saw it as a "rare TV opportunity" where "the scriptwriters [were] released from the shackles" to "explore more completely the make-up of their characters".[18]

One year after the *SITA* writers had been 'released' from the storyline, their characters were described as "the most uncharismatic on TV" with "unsubtle dialogue" and "trite, plotting...soap – not drama".[19] And if, finally, as AWG advocate David Rapsey argued, the *SITA* storyline dispute was all about getting "better television,"[20] then alas the strategy would appear to have failed.

And as a post-script to the question of who "authors" a TV serial, it is curious that, while the National Film and Sound archive lists Roger Simpson as the co-writer of virtually all 320 episodes of *SITA* (and it's true he created the concept, many of the characters and the "story engine") but in the estimation of the Australian Writer's Guild, the AWGIE for best script of a TV Serial of 2000 went to...

Paul Davies breaks off reading out his paper...
PAUL DAVIES: Just let me check...
He bends down and picks up a large silver nib-like sculpture (an actual "AWGIE"). He holds it out in front of him, reading off the inscription.
PAUL DAVIES: Ah Yes... it looks like there's only *one* credited writer engraved here for Episode 34 *Return of the Prodigal*...
He holds the Awgie up next to his face, the camera moves in, he smiles.
PAUL DAVIES: (humbly) Thank you so much...It's a great honour.

[17] Hughes, Simon. "Soap In Hard Water" *The Age* (13/3/2000): 7. Print.
[18] Perkin, Corrie. "*Bellbird*, Recast and Revisited" *The Age* (16/1/2000): 16. Print.
[19] Hooks, Barbara. "TV Highlights" *The Age Green Guide* (1/3/2001): 28. Print.
[20] Middendorp, Chris. "Drama Behind The Scenes" *The Age Green Guide* (13/7/200): 14. Print.